The wind sang dolefully among the boulders and whipped the rain into the face of the man hurrying up the mountainside. The broad brim of his hat drooped and the hem of his cloak flapped dismally around his ankles.

Lightning creased the sky, briefly bleaching his face as white as his dog-collar. The ensuing clap of thunder shook the ground beneath his feet and rolled away to silence. He glanced nervously up at the clouds and quickened his pace.

Clambering over slippery rocks and stumbling through runnels of rushing water, he seemed oblivious to the cold and wet. Only when he scrambled up a last muddy bank and found himself standing on a flat, rain-washed plateau did his features betray any emotion. Before him, the shadowy bulk of a ruined castle loomed out of the night, its silhouette black against the dull pewter of the sky. A hint of grim satisfaction flickered across his face.

He crossed the drawbridge cautiously, wary lest the rotting planks might crack beneath his weight, and passed under a lofty stone arch into an abandoned and overgrown courtyard. Seeking out an area free of weeds and fallen masonry he knelt down and produced two objects from within the folds of his cloak.

The first, a cloth-wrapped bundle, he put down by his side without a glance. The second, he handled with great care, even with reverence. It was a small wooden casket, banded with brass. He placed it on the ground before him and lifted the lid. Another flash of lightning lit up the night, allowing a brief glimpse of the interior. It was lined in scarlet satin, and was full of a fine grey powder. Raindrops pocked the surface of the dust.

The man picked up the bundle and rose to his feet. As he unwound the cloth a new sound joined the dirge of the elements; the cry of a creature in distress. He threw the swaddling aside and adjusted his load so that it lay in the crook of his

3

left arm. It was a baby, no more than a few days old, naked and screaming in protest against the biting cold.

The man's hand disappeared into the folds of his cloak and emerged, clasping the hilt of an ornate dagger. Lightning seared the sky. The blade gleamed.

"Prince of Darkness, I honour thee!" he shouted above the crash of the thunder. The baby redoubled its squalling.

"Master of Evil, I worship thee!" the wind tore at the man's cloak, as if nature itself was raging against his blasphemy. He raised the knife.

"Lord of Blood, I summon thee!"

The blade swept down and the credits rolled.

Dying for Hammer

Based on a fictional story

Directed by

Steve Manthorp

Starring, in order of appearance:

Ralph Bates	as Renwick
Andrew Kier	as Father Shandor
Michael Ripper	as Michael
Martita Hunt	asWidow Mordant
Toke Townley	as Tom
Veronica Carllson	as Constance Quigley
Roy Kinnear	as Burgomeister von Trapp
Oliver Reed	as Lawrence Talbot
Patrick Troughton	as Klove
Joan Sims	as Elsbieta
Peter Cushing	as the Baron
Roy Stewart	as Joachim
Carmen Munroe	as Dominique
Christopher Lee	as the Count

With Guest Appearances by

Ernest Thesiger as Doctor Pretorius

and

Turhan Bey as himself

(Please note that guest stars appear in black & white. Do not adjust your mind's eye)

Chapter 1

When Shandor came to release Michael, he found the old man asleep in the stocks. The Father looked down at him sadly. Sometimes he found it hard to believe that the Lord was present in all His works.

Michael looked as if he had been knocked together by a misguided amateur. His face was sallow and marbled with broken veins. What little hair he had left was grey, greasy and stuck out in tufts. His jaw hung slack, revealing a graveyard of discoloured and broken teeth. Shandor could smell him from several feet away.

But despite all this - and despite the fact that he was in the stocks for fouling Goodman Brockhaus's vegetable patch - there was still an air of innocence about him. It was a quality that never deserted Michael. It enveloped him like a cocoon, protecting him from the worst consequences of his actions, influencing the animate and inanimate in equal measure. If he fell out a tree (and Michael needed no good reason to be in one in the first place), his fall would be broken by a passing child: if he was in the stocks, nobody would throw anything at him. This being the case, there was little point in incarcerating him, other than a faint and fading hope that it might prove deterrent, and the brief respite that it offered to his liver.

Today, however, he had suffered more than nominal punishment. Merrythought, the gravedigger's dog, had taken advantage of the old man's helplessness to urinate down his back. Father Shandor was not sure whether this had been an act of vengeance on the part of the dog for some specific grievance, or whether it was simply an act of arbitrary mischief, but he deplored it anyway, and had come to release Michael early.

At some time over the last few hours, the old man had been sick over himself. Shandor drew the locking pin from the stocks, lifted the crossbar and nudged Michael with his foot. The old man awoke coughing, and spat, hitting the priest's sandal.

"Time up already, Father? Don't it just fly?"

As he sat up, he noticed the pool of vomit in his lap.

"God's ballocks!" he exclaimed, "Begging your pardon, Father, but did you just do that? Been overdoing that sacremenstral wine, eh?" He gave the father a conspiratorial wink.

Whilst vomiting on consecrated ground was surely a greater sin than polluting the secular utility of Goodman Brockhaus's vegetable patch, Shandor felt that this was a time to exercise tolerance. He wiped his toe on the grass.

"I hope that you have had time to consider your actions, Michael, and repent."

"Oh hell aye, Father," said Michael, assuming what he hoped was an expression of contrition, "that's what I was doing just now, repenting an' that."

"Father," he continued after a penitent pause, "what with not being able to work today, I've not got a penny to feed the wife -"

It was all cobblers, of course. Michael had not done a day's work in years and the mother of his only child had not accepted a penny from him since immediately prior to the conception. Shandor reached for his purse anyway, and dropped a florin into Michael's grubby palm.

"Mind that you spend it on food, now," he said, without a great deal of conviction.

But Michael wasn't listening, either to the Father's words or to the lies he told in return. He tugged a greasy forelock, marshalled his flies and scuttled down the path.

* * *

Shandor strolled back to the Presbytery ruminating sadly upon Michael's son. He passed Renwick, his pale and solemn curate, who stood over Mole the gravedigger, supervising the digging of a grave for Philomena Blepp, daughter of Carter Blepp. Died of a wasting disease. At least that had not taken long, there not having been a great deal of baby Blepp to waste, but Shandor dreaded outbreaks of wasting diseases. There were worse ways to die, certainly, than from the erosion of the body. But there were wasting diseases and wasting diseases: erosions of the body and erosions of the soul. He genuflected.

"Throw a bucket of water over the stocks when you've done, Renwick," he said. Renwick nodded and Shandor passed on.

"Throw a bucket of water over the stocks when you've done, Mole," said Renwick.

Mole muttered something under his breath. Merrythought sensed that it was not a good time to be around his master, and slunk off to find a quiet corner of the graveyard in which to continue his slumber.

At the sound of the door Widow Mordant came scurrying out of the kitchen, wiping her hands on her apron.

"Doctor Pretorius called while you were out," she said stiffly, "I told him I didn't know when you would be back."

This was a lie. Widow Mordant had been well aware that Shandor had only left the presbytery to release Michael, but she did not approve of the Father's acquaintance with Pretorius. He drank too much, smoked foul cigars and smelled of brimstone.

"He said that he had something to discuss with you."

11

In more propitious circumstances Shandor would have regarded this as a pleasant prospect. Pretorius was an educated man, a keen and iconoclastic disputant and a generous host. But the events of the afternoon had conspired to weave a pall of gloom around the priest and at that moment he wanted nothing more than to eat a solitary supper and spend the rest of the evening reading in his study.

His housekeeper stood her ground and showed no inclination to return to the kitchen.

"Is there anything else?" Shandor asked wearily.

Widow Mordant paused for a moment, looking uncomfortable, then said archly, "he called me a name."

Shandor raised an eyebrow. Many and varied though Pretorius' faults might be, the Father had never thought of him as a spiteful man.

"What did he call you?" he asked.

"I couldn't say," she replied primly, only serving to fuel Shandor's curiosity.

"Well, did he use foul language?"

Much to the Father's surprise, the suggestion of a blush rouged the widow's cheeks.

"He - he called me his busty beauty."

Shandor was overcome with a sudden coughing fit. Whilst the ample proportions of Widow Mordant's front elevation were not in dispute, such a familiar description sat unhappily upon a woman who he tended to think of as a natural feature of the landscape; timeless, immovable and with craggy uplands.

The Father directed a line of appeasement at her puritanical nature.

"It's unforgivable, Agnes, quite unforgivable. I will have strong words with the Doctor about this."

12

He detected a slight softening in the granite of the widow's outrage.

"And after supper you may take the rest of the evening off to recover from this...unfortunate incident."

This was nominal benevolence, as Shandor had no intention of calling upon her services after supper anyway, but it had the desired effect. Widow Mordant turned and headed back to the kitchen with, Shandor thought, the slight hip-swing of a doughty widow recalling her youth.

* * *

The village of Karnstein lies like sediment in the bowl of the desolate Vale of Walach, overlooked on either side by the gothic towers of the two castles. It has a ruined abbey (the only inhabitable part of which is occupied by Doctor Pretorius), a church, a brothel, a market on Wednesdays and Saturdays, and a tavern. The road to Karnstein passes through the village then forks into two rutted cart tracks which snake up either side of the valley, both overgrown with weeds since people ceased visiting the castles. At this junction, the nearest Karnstein has to a crossroad, the Brethren, Walach's puritan forefathers, used to mete out summary justice of a weekend in lieu of any more frivolous entertainment. All that now remains to commemorate the memory of those brutal times is the Crow and Gibbet.

On this particular day, the sun shone down anaemically on the inn and twinkled off the diamond panes of its closed windows. The sign above the gimmer's bench hung still and silent. Nearby, the geese around the horse-trough sorted through the chaff spilled from the day's nosebags. It was easy to believe that the place was asleep.

When Michael walked in, however, he found Tom the innkeeper standing on a stool pouring a jug of water through a funnel into the barrel on the bar.

"Evening, Tom," said Michael.

"You're early tonight," replied Tom, frowning in concentration.

"Aye," agreed Michael. He approached the bar in amicable interest.

"What's that you're doing, then?" he asked.

"Just topping up the beer," replied Tom.

Michael reached up and straightened the funnel.

"Well, isn't that a wonderful thing?" he said, impressed. "I never knew you could do that."

At that moment, Tom's nostrils flared in protest as they caught the full heady bouquet of Michael's organic odours. He recoiled with a cry, lost his footing and disappeared headlong behind the bar. There was a crash and a thud, and a spray of water spattered the wall.

Michael leaned over the counter and peered down at Tom, who lay in a pool of water amid jagged shards of earthenware, clutching the back of his head.

"Are you all right, Tom?" he asked.

"Am I all right?" asked Tom, "Am I all fucking right? You come in here covered in fucking puke and smelling like a three-day-old fucking piss-pot! You bring half the fucking flies in the fucking valley with you! You break my fucking pitcher, not to mention my fucking skull, and then you have the fucking gall to ask me if I'm all fucking right?"

"It's not my puke, it's the Father's," Michael muttered defensively.

"I don't care if it's the fucking Pope's, I don't want it on my fucking floor!"

A moment later Michael flew out of the door, described a short, graceless arc and landed face first beside the horse-trough.

"And don't come back until you've fucking washed!" Tom roared over the hysterical cackle of the geese, and slammed the door.

14

Michael lay face down in the mud for a while then rose unsteadily to his feet. He pressed the heel of his fist to his chin and examined it for blood, then opened his hand to enjoy the comforting gleam of the florin.

He turned his attention to his clothes. The vomit, which had been drying nicely, was now covered with a layer of that mud peculiar to horse-troughs, comprised in equal measure of oat-chaff, the excretions of sundry beasts of burden, late night pisses and little green sausages of goose-shit.

Sighing at the tragic inevitability of fate, Michael balanced his florin on the sill of the trough and climbed in.

* * *

The skies had darkened and ragged clouds drifted across the moon. In the public bar of the Crow and Gibbet a garrulous hubbub accompanied a grudge game of Bloody Fives. The last time they had played, Yeoman Muller had made a fool of himself by pinning his thumb to the table in the third round. The crowd around the trestle heckled and bet as John the Smith picked up the dagger and spread his fingers for the second round of the rematch. Around the walls the gimmers, widows and sots sipped their halves through toothless gums and observed the chaos indulgently.

Michael sat alone, engrossed in the game, chuckling into his beer and urging on the players with an impartial stream of vile epithets.

"G'arn with yer!" he was muttering, "G'arn, yer overstuffed donkeyfu – "

Michael was a little slow to notice the silence that suddenly had fallen upon the room and his words carried across to the gaming table. The Smith glared at him for a moment, and then turned his attention back to the door.

Michael followed his gaze and saw four young strangers huddled together nervously, framed against the night. With the instinct of the cadging cur that he was, he smiled ingratiatingly at the strangers. Only in his eyes, however, was there any welcome for them.

One of the four, a fat-faced man with spectacles, stepped forward and addressed Tom.

"Good evening, landlord," he said, "I wonder if you can help us. Our dwiver wefuses to take us any further. We need twansport - "

"- Not far," interjected one of the two female travellers, a pretty young woman in a brown travelling cape and fox-fur muff.

Tom picked up a wineglass and absently dirtied it on the corner of his apron.

"And where would you be going, Sir, that's not far?"

"Only to Castle Fw - "

The dagger missed the stranger's ear by a whisker and buried itself with a hum in the doorjamb. Michael glanced across to the gaming table. Everyone stood frozen, not betraying by the slightest flicker of an eye which of them had thrown it.

When Michael looked back, Von Trapp, the Burgomeister stood behind the strangers. He spoke, and the smaller of the two women started in surprise.

"Nobody lives at the Castle," he said, casually wrenching the dagger out of the wood. The Burgomeister was a short, balding, fat man; every bit as unfit as he looked, but with a good deal of natural strength.

"But he is my - " said the other gentleman, a big framed, muscular specimen. He started to pull an envelope from an inside pocket. The Burgomeister's hand snapped down over his wrist like a bear-trap.

"Nobody lives at the Castle!" he repeated with a cold certainty that forbade dissent.

16

The entrance of Von Trapp took the matter out of the commoners' hands. Conversation returned, subdued and sullen, to the tables. Nobody cared to ask the Burgomeister for the dagger back, and the Fives game was abandoned.

Michael lifted his tankard, but was annoyed to see a fly vibrating in desperate circles around the surface of his beer. He reached into the stein with stubby fingers.

Von Trapp ordered cold meat, bread and wine, and led the four to the only empty table in the tavern. Taking the corner bench, the two women edged past the horrid, wet old derelict who sat nearby, endeavouring to stuff his hand into his tankard. The men sat on either side of the Burgomeister.

Von Trapp immediately started to question the party. After a few moments' hissed conversation the man without spectacles produced the envelope again and handed it over. While the Burgomeister read, Michael took advantage of the lull in the conversation.

"Excuse me, Miss," he said to the woman beside him. He waited. She must have failed to hear him, he thought. He tugged gently at her cloak. She flinched.

"Piss off, Michael," said the Burgomeister testily. He finished the letter and resumed his interrogation, which was shaping up into an argument with the muff-woman. Michael stared glumly at the fly.

The dispute grew more heated until finally the Burgomeister, who was not renowned for his self-control, leapt to his feet. Wagging his finger at the muff-woman he shouted, "- and there's no-one in the village stupid enough to take you!"

He clambered ungainly over the bench and stood up.

"I suggest that you and your friends are on the mail coach to Prague tomorrow afternoon! Goodnight, Miss Quigley," he hissed and stalked out, leaving in his wake the second pregnant silence of the evening. After what he estimated to be a decent pause, Michael broke it.

"Excuse me, Miss," he ventured, "can I borrow that there pointy thing?"

Miss Quigley regarded him for a moment with an expression normally reserved for the sort of lower invertebrate she might find in a salad; but finally plucked the pin from her muff and offered it to him.

Michael lowered the sequined end into his pot. The fly, which had by now reviewed its short life and was making its peace with the Lord of the Flies, did not question the miracle that had deposited this twinkling life raft beside it, but swam over with alacrity and clambered aboard. Michael withdrew the pin, flicked the fly onto the floor and trod on it. He sucked the pin dry and handed it back to its owner.

"Would you be wanting a guide to Castle Frankenstein, then, Miss?" he asked, disingenuously.

Chapter 2

"You stupid old man!" shouted the other woman.

The strangers had been obliged to stay in the Crow and Gibbet into the small hours of the morning, watching Michael drink himself into an almost transcendental stupor at their expense. When Tom's fatigue had finally exceeded his avarice and he had thrown them out, they had been further delayed while Michael had repeatedly vomited in the horse trough.

Shortly after they had started climbing the hill, it had started to rain; not heavily, but steadily and with a commendable quiet efficiency. The path had been steep and muddy and the woman without a muff was not dressed for the conditions. Her cloak and the hem of her skirts had soon become sodden and heavy, and she had slipped frequently.

She had lost count of the number of times the four of them had huddled together in silent misery while Michael had stumbled off into the trees to relieve himself. Once he had been gone for so long that they had begun to suspect he had deserted them. After a search, during which the woman without a muff had scratched her face on a thorn, they had discovered him feet first, snoring under a bush.

But at last they had stood, bedraggled and shivering, between stone gateposts, looking across an ancient drawbridge at the decayed splendour of a castle.

Michael had drawn their attention to it with a flamboyant sweep of his hand.

"Behold!" he had announced grandly, "Castle Frankenstein."

The woman without a muff had peered through the drizzle. Above the entrance, carved into the granite arch, was a crest; a bar sinister dividing a bat and a serpent, supported by two wyverns rampant, and below it, in letters fully three feet high, the legend 'Drakul'.

"You stupid old man!" she repeated bitterly, "You miserable cretin!"

"What's the matter?" asked Michael in bewilderment.

The man who didn't wear spectacles grabbed Michael by the throat and pointed up at the crest with a trembling finger.

"What's the matter?" he shouted, "what's the bloody matter? Can't you read?"

"No," replied Michael pathetically. He could feel the prospect of reward trickling like the rain down his neck and disappearing.

"Oh, Chwist," said the other man, removing his spectacles and leaning back against the gatepost. Far across the valley, barely visible through the rain, a light winked in a window of one of the towers of Castle Frankenstein. The woman without a muff sat down on the drawbridge and started to cry. Miss Quigley crouched down beside her and put a comforting arm around her shoulders.

After a monumental effort, Michael's mistake dawned upon him. He slapped his forehead.

"Well, of all the daft mistakes!" he said. "I've only gone and brought you to the wrong castle, haven't I?"

A wet muff slapped him in the face and dropped into a puddle at his feet.

"Lor'y me!" he scoffed, "You must think I'm an old fool. Still," he added, hopefully, "you have to see the funny side."

At this point things got a little confused. Some powerful force - lightning, perhaps - knocked Michael to the ground. He was buffeted by several kicks and blows. When he had blinked the mud from his eyes, he found himself flat on his back with the unbespectacled man sitting on his chest. The man's fist - a good-sized, beefy fist and a credit to its owner, Michael noted - quivered above his face. In a world full of uncertainty, that fist seemed to be one inevitable truth. Michael screwed his eyes shut and waited.

"Good evening."

It was a quiet voice, nearby. Michael opened a tentative eye. The fist still trembled above his nose, but beyond it, silhouetted against the clouds, a figure leaned over them solicitously.

"Can I be of any assistance?" he asked. "My name is Renwick."

* * *

Michael was fast being forgotten. As the party poured out their catalogue of disaster to the curate, so his part in it was being reduced to that of a malevolent natural phenomenon, on a par with a small earthquake, or diarrhoea. He wasn't sorry about the general drift of conversation. He was well aware that no possibility remained of the strangers paying for his services and he knew that he had narrowly avoided a hiding. He could see no benefit to any of the parties present in reviving unpleasant memories.

Renwick offered the menfolk the surrogate warmth of a hip flask.

"You must stay the night at the castle," he said.

This was Michael's cue to depart. He didn't mind leading fools to the castle - either castle - but he was buggered if he would enter either himself. Both had evil reputations. He backed up to the wall and started to sidle along with affected nonchalance. Just when he thought that he had made good his escape, Renwick laid a casual hand upon his shoulder.

"You too, Michael," he said. "I'm sure that we can find a place for you by the kitchen hearth."

"Very kind, I'm sure, Herr Renwick," Michael mumbled. He couldn't help wondering who the 'we' might be who were occupying the ostensibly abandoned castle, "but I really has to go now."

The curate's grip tightened.

"I insist," he insisted. "The path is steep and treacherous."

"Let him go," said four-eyes, "With a bit of luck he might fall and bweak his wetched neck."

Michael agreed enthusiastically, but the curate was not to be deterred. With a gesture to the strangers and a firm grip on Michael's arm he led them across the drawbridge, up the steps and through a small door inset in the portcullis.

They crossed the gloomy courtyard in silence, making for a grand arched doorway. At their approach the doors swung open. The curate stood aside to let the gentlefolk enter, then propelled Michael through with a shove. Michael peered round the back of one of the doors to see who had opened them. There was no one there. He laughed nervously.

"How do they do that, then?" he asked, and was ignored.

They stood in the great hall, a vast and gloomy chamber lit by a pair of candelabrae placed at either end of a refectory table. Trails of cobweb dangled from the galleries above. Their footfalls raised whorls of dust.

The walls were decorated with antique weapons and faded tapestries. Miss Quigley peered at the one of the hangings, trying to make sense of the knots of human and sub-human figures; then turned away, appalled, when she succeeded.

The thought of negotiating the path back down to the village was becoming ever more attractive in Michael's mind.

"I will show Michael to the kitchen," announced Renwick, "then inform the Count that he has guests."

He raised a hand against the murmurs of protest.

"He keeps late hours, and enjoys fresh...company. He would not forgive me or himself if he did not entertain you personally."

The doors behind them swung shut with an emphatic thump, making Michael jump in surprise. He had barely landed before the curate had him by the arm and was leading him out of the hall, along a passage and through a succession of doors, each of which opened silently before them and closed clangorously behind.

They stopped at last at a low side door. Producing a large iron key from his pocket, Renwick unlocked the door, hurled Michael into the darkness and locked it immediately, muffling the old man's shriek.

* * *

Michael had not been expecting Renwick's shove in the back or the flight of steps on the other side of the door. He tumbled arse over end, coming to rest at the bottom flat on his back, surrounded by the fairy jingle of his loose change as it ran around the floor seeking out cracks and corners in which to hide.

"Ballocks!" he shouted.

It was a generous curse, ranged at the curate, the stairs, the loss of his money, and at life itself. He struggled to his feet and clambered back up the steps to the door. He explored its smooth surface then, when he failed to find a handle, beat upon the wood while spewing out a torrent of vile abuse. Finally accepting that nobody could hear him, he hobbled back down the stairs and set about exploring his prison.

He began to edge around the walls, hoping to discover another way out of the room or, failing that, a hearth in which there might remain some dull ember that could be blown back into flame.

Instead, he trod on a rat. It responded with an ear-piercing squeal and a flurry of bites and scratches to his ankle. Michael's bladder emptied in a warm stream down his leg, effecting a modest degree of revenge upon the rodent.

Half way along the second wall his hand fell into the void of a window casement. His heart leapt and he clambered up onto the deep sill to look down. He could just make out the sheer face of a cliff, plunging into unfathomable darkness.

"Ballocks," he muttered, and felt about himself for some object with which to plumb the distance to the ground. He briefly considered the one remaining groat in his pocket, but with a proper sense of priorities settled for one of his boots instead. He prised it off, dropped it into the void and waited, straining to hear it land. After a long minute's silence, he abandoned the window as a potential escape route and continued his peripatesis.

Before long, he found himself back at the bottom of the steps. Next, holding his arms straight out to protect himself from any obstacle he started across the room and almost immediately fell headlong over a low object.

"Spunkpigs!" he hissed, picking himself up and aiming a savage kick at the obstacle, forgetting that his boot was in all probability still falling towards Karnstein forest. Purple stars burst against the darkness. He howled with pain and hopped around, clutching his foot. When the agony had passed, he put a hand out into the darkness and felt for the object. It was a long, low box, about a foot high and a little longer than himself. He sat down on it.

24

He was cold and wet, ached in every limb, and suspected that he had broken his toe. He was miserable and scared. There was not a lot he could do about it, however. The lid of the box was dry at least, and taller than the average rat. Resigning himself to his lot, he lay down and made himself as comfortable as circumstances allowed. As he drifted off to sleep, his first dream was of hearing the faint echo of his boot as it landed in the valley below.

* * *

In the darkness, something stirred. It had been sleeping for hours, but now hunger spurred it to action.

It yawned and stretched, then put a pale hand to the velvet-covered surface above its head and pushed - and nothing. It pushed once more, harder, but again to no effect. Hissing its displeasure, it braced itself and heaved with both hands.

The lid creaked up slowly, and the object that had been weighing it down rolled off with a cry and landed heavily on the floor. Annoyed, the occupant of the box flung the lid back on its hinges.

Rising bewildered from the floor, Michael caught the lid squarely on the back of the head and went down again. Momentarily under the impression that the man without spectacles had sought him out in order to continue his attack, Michael staggered to his feet, wailing apologies and protecting his head with both arms. When a short wait had brought no further assault, he peered cautiously through the crook of his elbow.

In the short time he had been asleep, the rain had stopped and the clouds had moved on to spoil somewhere else's dawn. A plump moon, waxing towards the full, shone through the window, casting just enough light for Michael to see that there was no sign of the four-eyed bastard. In fact, the room was empty but for three boxes similar to the one upon which he had been sleeping.

Michael looked down. In the box in front of him lay a beautiful woman in a diaphanous low-cut nightgown, staring back at him. When at last he managed to tear his attention from her cleavage, Michael couldn't help noticing that she didn't look best pleased.

She sat up slowly, not taking her eyes from Michael's for a moment.

"I'm, er...I'm, er...I'm,er..." he could hear his own voice, as if from far away, "I'm, er..." it trailed away to silence.

The woman rose to her feet and stepped gracefully out of the casket. Michael stood goggle-eyed and blinking as she advanced upon him.

As she approached, Michael realised that the glint in her eyes was not annoyance – or at least, not solely so – but a rapacious hunger. So that was it: many times in the past, Michael had salivated to tavern tales of haughty aristocratic beauties slaking their lust upon virile peasant bucks, and God's ballocks, if it wasn't about to happen to him. He swallowed. He wished he hadn't wet himself earlier. Still, his trousers were almost dry now and she probably wouldn't notice; of if she did, maybe she would find it rustic.

A crash nearby made him jump as the lid of a second box was thrown open. Two more crashes followed in immediate succession. Three pallid beauties clambered out of their unorthodox boudoirs. Michael wondered at the eccentricities of the ruling classes.

"One at a time please, ladies, I've plenty to go round," he croaked, backing into the corner.

The first woman was very near now and he could not help noticing that, close to, she did not quite sustain the initial impression she had made upon him. Her hair was a mess for a start. Her nightgown, too, was soiled and torn. Most off-putting of all was the rash of sores covering her neck and cleavage. The idea of being a plaything of the decadent aristocracy did not seem quite so appealing.

But it was too late. Suddenly they were all over him, clawing the shirt off his back and showing not the least inclination to worship at the temple of his body in turn. Michael sighed in resignation and slid his hand up the nearest nightdress.

"Off!" hissed one of the women, grasping his wrist with altogether unexpected strength. She effortlessly pulled his hand off his thigh and wrenched it up in front of his face.

"Dirty old man," she said, and broke his forefinger.

Another hand clamped over his mouth and muffled his scream. His attacker threw back her head and laughed. Michael could not help but be impressed by the ivory whiteness and length of her incisors. Then she wrenched his head back and threw herself upon his exposed neck.

It took them about five minutes to empty him. At first they squabbled like animals over his jugular, but before long each settled down to her own artery and commenced feeding in earnest. After the first few savage bites and the pain when they jostled his broken finger, Michael did not have much idea what was going on. His dying thought was that he was cold, infinitely cold.

Existing as they had done for many years exclusively on blood, the brides of Dracula (for such they were) had virtually no resistance to the effects of alcohol. Even several hours after leaving the Crow and Gibbet enough beer continued to course through Michael's bloodstream to get the four of them quite squiffy. They arose from their feast giggling and unsteady and proceeded to disport themselves with an utter absence of the dignity traditionally associated with their kind. In the midst of their horseplay one fell headlong over Michael's stiffening corpse.

"Yuck!" she complained. "It smells of wee!"

"Le'sh get rid of it," said her companion.

"Chuck it out of the window," suggested the third.

Taking a limb each, the Brides staggered over to the window and took up position.

"One!" they counted, swinging the body.

"Two!"

On three, they hurled it into the night. One Bride sat down with a bump on the floor.

"I don't feel very well," she said.

Bouncing off the jagged cliff-face, Michael's corpse plummeted towards Karnstein forest.

Chapter 3

Michael woke up feeling like death. He lay perfectly still, afraid that any sudden movement might be his last. He had a raging thirst and his skull seemed to have been swapped in the night for another, several sizes too small. His breathing was constricted, as if some heavy animal was asleep on his chest. He opened a tentative eye. It was a badger.

Michael screamed. The badger leapt into the air and landed with its claws outspread. Michael bellowed again and swiped at it. The badger, which had taken Michael's gently rolling stomach for a natural feature of the landscape placed there by a benevolent God for its own convenience, did not stop to question what it had done in the night to change God's mind, but turned tail and fled.

Michael sat up and looked around blearily. Behind him a craggy cliff rose into the blue morning sky. Ahead, the startled badger disappeared into thick forest. It had been years since he had even tried to recall the events of the nights-before-the-mornings-after: the progressive pickling of his brain and metaphysical laws far beyond his feeble ken had conspired to condemn him to a perpetual present, with little short-term memory and no interest in the future.

He struggled to his feet and closed his eyes to the inevitable wave of nausea. When it had passed, he looked down, and saw that he had been lying in an indentation moulded to every contour of his spread-eagled body. In anybody else, this would have been a matter of curiosity and concern. But Michael was possessed of a degree of stupidity and intellectual laziness far beneath the capacities of the least of humankind.

A few yards away his boot lay in a similar depression of its own. He limped over to it and pulled it on. He coughed and spat, scratched his bottom and the faint scars on his neck, and then hobbled off into the forest.

It was a perfect morning in Karnstein forest. The sun shone down through emerald green leaves and threw dappled light onto the forest floor. Birds trilled in the trees and rabbits frolicked in the bracken. A deer skittered across his path. Michael wished that they would shut up and fuck off.

It wasn't long before he stumbled upon a path. Thinking of the jug of beer that awaited him at the end of his journey he perked up a little, and set off in what seemed the more promising direction.

Before long, a brook babbled into view. Michael broke into a run, flung himself down on the bank and started to drink noisily. Every living thing within earshot took flight. Every living thing but one, anyway.

When at last, after having imbibed copious quantities of water, a pebble and several Caddis-fly larvae, Michael lifted his head out of the stream to breathe, a voice close to his ear enquired,

"Are you of my kind?"

For the third time in as many minutes Michael yelled, and leapt to his feet.

"Eh?" he enquired.

The stranger, who had been kneeling beside him, rose too.

"Are you hairy...on the inside?" he asked.

Michael peered at him suspiciously, wondering what he was on about. From the stranger's accent it was obvious that he a foreigner. He was athletic, broad-shouldered and nattily dressed. He carried a travelling bag and an alpenstock. His hat had a blue feather inserted in the band.

Michael looked him up and down, and came to the wildly improbable conclusion that the man was a catamite on the pick-up.

"Dirty bugger," he muttered darkly, "never you bloody mind where I'm hairy." The stranger laughed.

"I fear that we are at crossed purposes, sir," he said, "you are obviously not of the fraternity I took you for, and I certainly do not embrace the proclivities you seem to suspect. If I did," he added, "I assure you that I would rather commit the sins of Sodom on a bear with haemorrhoids before I considered your diseased flesh."

"That's all right then," replied Michael, relaxing a little, "just so long as we understand each other. You don't come from around these parts, do you, master?"

"I do not," the stranger replied. "No, sir, I hail from the United States of America. Virginia, to be precise."

Michael nodded wisely, though for what the stranger's words meant to him, he could have talking Swahili.

"Tell me," the young man continued, "do you know how far it is to the village of Karnstein?"

Whilst backward in almost every respect that defined intelligence, Michael was never slow to spot an opportunity.

"Karnstein...aye, I think I could guide you to Karnstein. T'would cost you sixpence, though."

The stranger reached into his pocket and tossed a coin into the air.

"Lay on, MacDuff," he said.

"It's Michael, master," said Michael, swiftly pocketing the coin.

"Lay on, Michael. My name is Lawrence Talbot."

The name rang a distant bell. Michael paused, trying to recollect where he had heard it before. After an unproductive moment he gave up and set off.

Michael had been right about the path, and before long it joined the cart track which led to Karnstein. They were on the wrong side of Hobb Crag, and the road climbed steeply up through Devil's Crack. At the top of the pass, Michael stopped, out of breath. Lawrence Talbot halted beside him and looked down into the Vale of Walach.

This morning it looked as attractive as it was ever going to. The early mist had cleared, and the road ahead wound down into the valley. On either side, sunlight glanced off the tracery of streams and rivulets which veined the surface of Walach Mire. Ravens croaked dolefully at each other from blasted trees.

The two stood shoulder to shoulder, Talbot pondering on the twisted destiny that had brought him here, Michael wondering whether the Crow & Gibbet was open yet. They were about to set off again when Talbot looked back and spotted a wagon labouring up the hill. They waited for it to pull up beside them.

"Not too bad a morning," said Michael.

"Could be worse," replied the carter.

"Would you be bound for Karnstein?"

"And what of it if I was?"

"Would you give us a lift?"

"You can climb on for five groats apiece."

Michael looked at Talbot. Talbot reached dutifully for his purse. They clambered up into the back of the wagon and sat down upon a long wooden crate. The carter snapped the reins against the horses' flanks and set off down the hill.

The cart picked up speed fast and before long, passengers and crate were bouncing dangerously around the back. Talbot tapped one of the many FRAGILE signs stencilled in red on the sides of the box.

"W-What is in the c-crate?" he shouted above the clatter.

"D-don't know," replied the carter, "s-smells rotten, though, and it w-weighs a b-bloody ton. I'm d-delivering it to some d-doctor."

"P-pretorius?" suggested Michael.

"T-that's the one," bellowed the carter, "all the w-way from E-egypt, it is."

He cracked the reins again and urged the horses on.

They maintained their pace across the Mire, and the horses were still galloping as they approached the outskirts of the village. As they turned the blind corner before Farkle Bridge, the carter was horrified to see a bizarrely clad figure standing directly in their path. He pulled frantically on the reins, but the horses were travelling too fast to stop. Just when it seemed inevitable that they must hit the man, the horses shied away, left the road and mounted the embankment. As the wheels hit the bank, the shaft broke with an earsplitting crack and the cart was flung up into the air like a catapult.

Michael was still wondering why the dusky figure in the middle of the road should be wearing a flowerpot on his head, when he found himself hurtling through the air. He was not alone. Flying in formation to his left was Talbot, and to the right, the crate. A moment later, all three plunged into the Farkle with a force that knocked all the wind out of Michael's lungs and replaced it with water.

Too dazed to swim, even had he known how, he spiralled slowly down towards the riverbed. He had almost lost consciousness when a hand grabbed him by the collar and pulled him up. After giving him a moment to draw breath, Talbot swam towards the bank, dragging the spluttering Michael behind him.

They dragged themselves out of the river and Michael collapsed onto all fours, retching up prodigious quantities of water. Talbot clambered up the bank and looked around. The cart, or what was left of it, lay a yard or two from the edge of the bank. But of the stranger in the road, the horses and the carter there was no sign.

* * *

Despite the sunshine a pall of gloom hung over Karnstein. Tom stood at the door of the Crow and Gibbet, broom in hand, staring up at Castle Dracula. He was by no means the only villager who had lain awake until dawn listening to the distant screams issuing from the castle.

He swept the detritus of the previous night into the road with a desultory flick of his broom. As he did, something bright amongst the rubbish caught his eye. He bent down and picked it up. It was a muff-pin. He looked back up at the castle. The young lady would have no need of it where she had gone, he thought, and dropped it into his pocket.

"What have you got there?" barked an imperious voice.

Tom glanced around guiltily. It was Von Trapp, clad in the black that denoted that he was employed in his official capacities as upholder of law and order and as village bully. He carried a blunderbuss under one arm and had a face like thunder.

"Nothing of value, Burgomeister," stammered Tom, fumbling in his pocket and producing the pin, "just this."

34

Von Trapp snatched it from the publican and turned it slowly. Each sequin caught the sunlight in turn, flashing him a message in some enigmatic morse code.

"This belonged to the Quigley woman."

"Yes, Burgomeister." Von Trapp pocketed the pin.

"How late did she and her companions linger here last night?"

"Late Burgomeister, very late. I tried to persuade them to stay."

Von Trapp grunted.

"Did they leave alone?" he asked.

Tom wavered between unwarranted loyalty to Michael and an entirely justified fear of the Burgomeister. Fear won. He was on the verge of telling all when the divine intervened in the person of His agent on earth.

"What happened last night?" asked Shandor, striding up to the pair, "I heard screams from the castle."

The arrival of the Father annoyed Von Trapp, who did not believe that there was any place for the guardian of the village's spiritual welfare in matters of law.

"Please do not trouble yourself, Father," he said, "I am investigating the matter myself."

Shandor ignored him.

"Who went up there?" he asked Tom.

"Strangers," interrupted the Burgomeister, struggling to remain polite, "nobody from your flock."

"Four of them," added Tom, avoiding Von Trapp's frosty glare, "they arrived by coach last night. Said they wanted transport to Castle Frankenstein. One of them had a letter, didn't she, Burgomeister?"

Shandor turned back to Von Trapp, whose patience was by now threadbare.

"With all due respect, Father," he growled, "this is not a matter for your concern."

Shandor's eyes flashed. He pointed up the hill with a trembling finger.

"That makes it my concern! If there was even the slightest suggestion that it had started again - "

"Now hold on! Just because there was a bit of a rumpus up at the castle doesn't mean..."

The Burgomeister trailed off into silence. He was staring over the priest's shoulder at a pair of draught horses which were limping exhaustedly up the street towards them. Behind them followed a humbly clad figure. Von Trapp hailed him. The carter made no reply, but continued to stare vacantly ahead. The horses drew level and the Burgomeister tried again. As the horses passed them Shandor gasped and genuflected.

"You'll not be getting anything out of that poor bugger," said Tom.

Neither riding nor walking, the carter hung in mid-air behind the horses, impaled on the splintered wooden shaft that entered his stomach and emerged, dripping red, from his back.

* * *

By the time Michael and Talbot had dried off and walked the last league into Karnstein, a crowd had gathered outside the Crow and Gibbet. Already unnerved by the events of the previous night, the appearance of a strange corpse, skewered like a kebab between two wild-eyed horses, had thrown the villagers into a superstitious frenzy.

There was a feeling amongst the crowd that the horses had a lot to answer for, and that they were best disposed of. The Burgomeister was making a stand, partly against superstition and ignorance, and partly because he reckoned that he had salvage rights on the animals. The way the argument was going, however, things were not looking good for the horses.

"Look at their staring eyes!" Granny Blepp was screeching. "They be agents of the Devil!"

"Probably demons themselves, got up as horses," added a voice from the crowd, to general assent.

Michael, who had been worming his way into the throng, finally broke through the front line and saw the horses.

"So that's where them buggers got to," he said, then caught sight of the deceased carter.

"Gawd and all his frigging angels!" he exclaimed, "begging your pardon, Father. But he's going to need more than a bread poultice, ain't he?

"I wouldn't mind," he lied after a moment's thought, "but he owed me money."

Michael looked around the crowd, staking his claim to the ten groats that were nestling, he knew, in the dead carter's waistcoat pocket. So far he had been blithely unaware of the effect his easy familiarity with the demon horses and the rapidly stiffening corpse had been having on everyone. There was a brief, stunned silence; then he was bombarded with questions from all sides.

"Who was he?"

"Where does he hail from?"

"How did he die?"

Michael gazed around bemusedly.

"Quiet! All of you!" roared the Burgomeister. "This is an official investigation, and I will ask the questions."

The cacophony subsided, and he turned back to Michael.

"Now, Michael; tell me everything you know about the deceased."

Michael was beginning to enjoy the attention.

"Now let me see..." he cupped his chin in his hand and frowned with the effort of recalling the events of the last hour, "...the diseased was a carter."

Von Trapp had been expecting a bit more than this.

"And how did you meet him?" he asked patiently.

"He gave me and Herr MacDuff a lift into the village."

"Talbot," corrected a voice from the back of the crowd. The villagers turned as one to gawp at the stranger.

"Not MacDuff. Lawrence Talbot at your service, sir."

"Talbot?" repeated Von Trapp. "That is a name I had never heard before last night."

Talbot stepped forward eagerly.

"My fiancé's party has arrived, then? Miss Quigley and her companions? Where are they? I must see them right away."

The Burgomeister's head was starting to swim. He was by temperament a slow, methodical man, with a love of order. Since last night, however, events quite beyond his control seemed to have overtaken him and were continuing to develop unpredictably and at an increasingly frenetic pace.

He was almost grateful when Granny Blepp intervened.

"You'll not see theys again, not alive!" she cackled, with the cheery sympathy for which her name was a byword in the village.

"What do you mean?" asked Talbot.

"Young man," said Father Shandor, "your fiancé and her party may be in grave peril. And yes, we cannot discount the possibility that they might even be dead."

" - Or worse," added Granny Blepp with gloomy satisfaction.

Talbot swayed for a moment as if on the verge of collapse, then gripped Shandor violently.

"Why?" he demanded.

"Last night your friends climbed up to Castle Dracula - "the dreaded name sparked off a sizzle of whispers and a flutter of genuflections amongst the villagers.

" - Dracula?" interrupted Talbot. "But Connie was to plead my case with the Baron at Castle Frankenstein."

The crowd grew even more restive at the mention of the other castle.

"She'd have fared no better there," Granny Blepp muttered darkly.

Von Trapp decided that it was time to regain control.

"The Baron has not lived at the castle for many years!" he exclaimed. "I explained that to your fiancé when I spoke with her last night."

"But why did they visit this Castle Dracula?" asked Talbot, ignoring the Burgomeister.

"Perhaps they entered by mistake," replied Shandor.

"And why do you believe that they are in danger?"

Shandor hung his head.

"We heard...screams in the night. The castle has an evil reputation. The last Count was a monster - more devil than man. The villagers fear that he has somehow found a way to return from... from whence they sent him."

"I must go to them!" declared Talbot. He looked up at Hob Crag, then over the village rooftops towards the other castle.

"Who will show me the way?" he asked.

There was a long silence. Michael developed a sudden interest in the toe of his boot.

"Very well," said Talbot, "if you are all too yellow to guide me I will go alone."

"Absolutely not! I forbid it!" roared Von Trapp, raising his blunderbuss.

"Smith! Muller! Hold him!"

It took the combined strength of four of Karnstein's burliest citizens to overpower the stranger, who kicked and fought with almost supernatural strength. When at last they held him, purple-faced and struggling, the Smith asked, "What should we do with him now?"

"Put him in the cell," commanded the Burgomeister.

"Herr Talbot, I am placing you under arrest for your own protection," he said, "take him away."

The Smith and his companions led the still protesting Talbot down the street. Michael watched them go. When they had disappeared around the corner he turned to Tom.

"Any chance of a pint, then, Tom?" he asked.

Chapter 4

It was never sensible for Michael to drink on an empty stomach. Faced with limited resources, though, ale had to take priority over food. By mid-afternoon, he was blind drunk and had run out of money.

He staggered out of the Crow & Gibbet and blinked in the unaccustomed sunlight. Much to his disappointment the horses and the body of the carter had gone, leaving behind a crimson puddle at which the pub cat was lapping surreptitiously. Michael had by now managed to convince himself that he had a legitimate claim to the dead man's small change, and had emerged with the intention of claiming it. He aimed a savage kick at the cat and missed. All was not yet lost, though. Even befuddled by drink, he had a good idea where the body would now be resting, awaiting a pauper's burial. Pausing only to urinate in the horse trough, he stumbled off towards Bumblewicz the Joiner's workshop.

As the village carpenter, it fell upon Herr Bumblewicz to make coffins for all but the dearest of Karnstein's departed. Over the years, he and his wife had expanded the business to include the laying-out, for which purpose they had adapted an unused potting shed adjoining the workshop. In this euphemistically named Chapel of Rest, the body of the carter lay flat on its back, staring up at the ceiling through sightless eyes.

Had it sat up and looked over its shoulder, it would have been able to see the room's only window, a small fanlight set above the door. In all probability it would also have given Michael a heart attack, as he was currently standing on an upturned bucket, peering in through the grimy pane of that very window.

As he was incapable of balancing upon an upturned bucket for long even when sober, Michael had no right to look quite as surprised as he did when it suddenly disappeared from under his feet. He fell to the ground with a squawk, a loud ripping and a clang as his face rediscovered the bucket.

"Shh!" he urged himself in a stage whisper.

He clambered to his feet. His trouser leg was torn from ankle to crotch. It flapped open, exposing his knee to the daylight for the first time in several months. He sighed.

The door to the Chapel of Rest was not locked. It was the work of a moment to slip inside and close it behind him. The body of the carter lay upon an old oak refectory that served as a laying-out table when it was not being used for Sunday dinner. Michael surveyed it uneasily. It was by no means the first dead body that he had come across - not even the first he had stolen from, corpse-robbing having been a bit of a money-spinner during the Cholera epidemic a few summers ago - but it was certainly one of the messiest. The ragged wound in its stomach, its blood-soaked jerkin and the vacancy of its unblinking eyes all conspired to make it the deadest looking corpse he had seen in a long time. He shuddered.

Michael was not by Karnstein's standards a superstitious man though, and a moment later, he was rifling expertly through the corpse's pockets. They were empty.

"Thieving pillock," he muttered under his breath.

Bumblewicz had wasted no time in stripping the body of everything of value. All it had left to its unknown name were the clothes it lay in. Even Michael would no longer consider stealing the jerkin in its present state. The breeches were all right, though, quite new and only a little bloody. Michael looked down at his own trousers. The wrinkled tip of his penis winked back at him coyly from within.

He lifted his jerkin and struggled with the knotted twine that served as a belt. His trousers dropped around his ankles and he stepped out of them.

Rigor Mortis had already worn off, leaving the corpse limp and unmanageable. Michael unbuckled its belt and tugged at the breeches, but couldn't get them over the carter's ample hips. He rolled it over onto its stomach and tried again, but with no more success.

He tucked its heels under his arms and dragged the body inch by inch towards him. When its hips were clear of the refectory he lets its legs drop to the floor, leaving the corpse doubled over the edge of the table, face down. He started working the breeches down over the carter's bottom with both hands.

"Lard-arsed bastard", he grumbled, as the fabric strained across the carter's buttocks. With an exasperated jerk, he finally managed to pull the breeches down around the corpse's ankles. In the process, however, he had edged the body a fraction too far, and it started to slither off the edge of the refectory. He hooked his arms under its armpits and strained to bunk it back up onto the tabletop.

For a few seconds there was no sound but the grunts accompanying his exertions. Then he heard the door creak behind him. Swallowing unhappily, he peered over his shoulder. In the doorway stood Herr Bumblewicz and beside him, slack-jawed in disbelief, his wife. Michael made a weak attempt at an ingratiating grin.

"I can't get it back up," he said, by way of explanation.

By way of reply, Dame Bumblewicz began to scream.

* * *

"Hail, fellow, and well-met," greeted Talbot from his cot as Michael was hurled into the cell.

"Evening, Herr Talbot," replied Michael from the floor. Behind him, the Burgomeister slammed the cell door and turned the key in the lock.

"You're a bloody disgrace!" he said, stabbing a finger through the bars. "This time you've gone too far. I'm going to teach you the error of your ways if you have to stay here until you rot."

He turned and strode out of the room, ignoring the entreaties and abuse that Talbot hurled at his back.

Talbot helped Michael to his feet.

"So what have you been doing to land up in here, friend?" he asked.

"Just a bit of a misunderstanding," replied Michael, tentatively touching the puffy swelling around his left eye.

He had eventually managed to persuade Von Trapp that his interest in the body of the carter had not been necrophiliac, but not before Bumblewicz had blacked his eye for giving his wife the vapours. In order to establish his innocence of the greater offence he had been obliged to admit the lesser one of attempted corpse-robbing, a serious enough crime in its own right. On the positive side, before the authorities had arrived to drag him away he had managed to struggle into the carter's breeches. He looked down at them through his good eye and picked fastidiously at a small clot.

Talbot settled back on his cot and Michael lowered himself onto the other, hitching up his breeches to prevent bagging the knees. Von Trapp had built the cell to hold two, although it had served to accommodate up to twenty after weddings. It was fitted out with all the modern conveniences: iron cots, a barred window and even a piss-pot.

44

The other half of the room was sparsely furnished with an interrogation desk and chairs, and a cupboard containing gaolers' requisites. The Burgomeister had built the cell at his own expense in order to contain serious offenders awaiting the prison cart or worse, and not least to give him the opportunity to impose modest custodial sentences of his own. It was his contribution to the civilising process of Law, and he was justifiably proud of it. When he returned to the building a few minutes later with a tray bearing a loaf of bread and a jug of water he was calm, and had the pacific air of a man indulging his pastime. He slid the tray under the door.

"When are you going to let me out?" asked Talbot, rising and approaching the bars. "Or are you happy to leave Connie and my friends in mortal danger from this maniac aristocrat? In my country a fancy title doesn't count for a good God damn."

"The Count is dead!" snapped Von Trapp, "as to your freedom, that depends on the answers you give me now."

He walked over to the table, sat down, took up a quill and opened his interrogation ledger.

"What was the nature of the medical matter that Miss Quigley had hoped to pursue with the late Baron?"

Talbot realised that he was more likely to secure his early release by co-operating with the Burgomeister.

"Her brother is a good friend of Frankenstein's nephew; he studied with him in Vienna. She was going to use the acquaintance to obtain an introduction. She hoped to persuade him to take me on as a patient."

"You, a patient? You look well enough to me."

"Mine is not an affliction of the body. I suffer from a periodic violent lunacy. At certain times of the month or when I am in distress, a fit comes over me. I lose all control over myself: I become savage, bestial."

He shuddered at the very thought of it.

"That is why I am obliged to travel a day behind Connie and her companions. For their safety, you understand.

"I have travelled the world in search of a cure, and sought the diagnosis of the best physicians and alienists, but to no avail. Although he chooses not to practise and shuns society, they say that Baron Frankenstein is the greatest medical genius alive. He is my last hope. If he cannot help me, then I no longer have any reason to live."

Overcome with emotion, Talbot blinked away tears to search for sympathy in the Burgomeister's features.

"But if Connie has sacrificed her life on my behalf," he continued, "then I would not wish to go on living anyway. I beg you, Burgomeister, man to man, let me go to her."

Despite appearances, Von Trapp was not a completely insensitive man; but despite - or perhaps because of - the effect Talbot's speech was having upon him, he was not prepared to see the young man throw his life away.

"I am sorry," he said, averting his eyes, "perhaps your fiancé is safe. Perhaps she and her companions spent an uncomfortable night in the ruins of Castle Dracula and cried out in their sleep. Heaven knows, a night in that place would be enough to give anybody nightmares.

"Why, even as we speak they are probably making their way down Hob Crag towards the village, and I'll wager that by tomorrow you will be teasing them about their misadventures, and planning other measures to manage your affliction. But until they do return, I cannot and will not release you."

"Then damn you!" exclaimed Talbot, slamming his fist against the bars and kicking the food-tray out of the cell. Michael stared wistfully after the bread as it spun across the floor.

The Burgomeister closed the ledger and stood up.

"I will review your case in the morning," he said stiffly, "Meanwhile I suggest that you try to get some sleep and learn to respect authority. Good night."

Talbot continued to look out through the bars for a while after Von Trapp had left. Finally he turned from the door and flung himself despondently onto his cot. Michael broke the ensuing silence with a nervous cough.

"You know you said you was a loony...?" he began, with all the tact he could muster.

* * *

As the sun lowered itself wearily behind Hob Crag, the shadows of the window bars lengthened across the recumbent form of Lawrence Talbot. Crouched on his cot, Michael kept a wary eye on the gentle rise and fall of his cell-mate's chest. Despite Talbot's reassurances that his lunatic fits were rare, Michael was taking no chances. By his side, he clasped the handle of the piss-pot, a weapon he was prepared to deploy at the slightest suggestion of eccentricity on Talbot's part.

His stomach growled. He tried, unsuccessfully, to recall the last time he had eaten. A ghostly memory flickered across the retina of his mind's eye of a feast shared with four pallid beauties in a moonlit room; but he dismissed it as the recollection of a wet dream.

From the far corner of the interrogation room, the abandoned loaf of bread sniggered at his discomfort. The sound annoyed him. If only he could persuade it to approach the cell door close enough for him to get his hands on it, he would wipe the smile off its crust.

He put the pot down, climbed off the cot and knelt beside the door.

"Here, bready-bready," he called softly, reaching a hand through the bars. The loaf regarded him suspiciously, its beady eyes gleaming in the shadows.

"Come here, nice bready," he coaxed, "Michael wants to eat you."

The loaf sniffed the air and shuffled forward a couple of inches.

"That's a good bready," continued Michael. "Bready come to daddy."

Cautiously, the loaf began to creep across the room towards Michael's outstretched hand, its farinaceous features alert to any sign of danger. When it was close enough, Michael allowed it to sniff at his fingers, then gently stroked its crusty flanks.

"Got you!" he exclaimed, grabbing it by the waist.

The loaf twisted and writhed in Michael's hand, but he had too firm a hold for it to break free. Ignoring its yeasty squeals he pulled it through the bars and looked it in the eyes.

"Who's laughing now, bastard?" he asked and raised it to his mouth. As he did, the crust split open and parted to reveal powerful jaws lined with row upon row of savage teeth. Michael shrieked in horror and relaxed his grip just enough for it to wriggle free and leap at him, burying its teeth in his shoulder...

"Wake up Michael!" urged Talbot, shaking him roughly. "Wake up, damn you!"

Michael awoke with a yell, leapt to his feet and collided with Talbot. The pot fell to the floor and shattered into a thousand pieces. He collapsed back onto his cot and rubbed his good eye.

"What do you want?" he asked blearily.

Whilst Michael had been asleep, the sun had set and the dusk dwindled into twilight. He peered at Talbot through the gloom, searching for any symptom of approaching mania.

"You must tie me up," Talbot replied. Michael stared at him blankly.

"Eh?"

Talbot started to unbutton his shirt.

"No time to explain," he muttered as his fingers worked feverishly. "We must tear my clothing into strips and you must use them to tie me to the cot."

Slowly the dawn of understanding broke over Michael's beetled brow.

"Now look here, Herr-dirty-bugger-Talbot, I thought we sorted out this business in the forest."

"Fool!" raged Talbot. He grasped Michael by the collar and pulled him to his feet.

"Don't you understand? It's starting!"

As he spoke, the rising moon bathed his contorted features in eerie blue light. He buried his face in his hands and turned away.

Aware that he was now defenceless, Michael took a more conciliatory tack.

"All right, all right: perhaps I could just tie your hands and feet. But no kissing or cuddling, and if any of this gets around the village I'll bloody have you, gentleman or not."

Talbot stumbled around the room, blind with pain. He fell against the cell door and beat his forehead against the bars. Michael winced.

"Come on now, young master, pull yourself together. I've said as how I'll do what you want."

He reached forward and touched Talbot on the shoulder.

"Get away from me!" Talbot snarled.

Michael backed off in confusion. Talbot leant against the cell door, his naked back pale in the moonlight. Michael could see the muscles beneath Talbot's skin writhing like moles in torment, and hear the creak of bone and the snap of sinew as his spine arched up and his shoulders broadened. His skin darkened as hair began to sprout wildly, covering his back in a sleek grey pelt.

Michael continued to back away until he felt the cold steel of the window bars behind him. Unable to take his eyes from the nightmare unfolding before him, he craned his head back and screamed for help.

In the Manor Library, the Burgomeister looked up from his book with a degree of grim satisfaction. It gave him no pleasure to deprive offenders of their liberty, as he was fond of explaining whilst in the process of doing so: his only reward was in releasing them back into society when they had learned their lesson. He was surprised that a single night's incarceration should have had such a dramatic effect upon an old lag like Michael, but he had seen too many hardened criminals fall apart at the merest whiff of the cell-house to give it much thought.

"Help!" Michael shrieked, "For fuck's sake, let me out!"

The lupine creature turned to see what was making all the noise. Its skull had narrowed and elongated, thrusting its snout forwards and extending its jaw. The same hair that had grown upon its body now covered its face and pointed ears. It drew back its lips and snarled.

50

"Oh God!" groaned Michael, flattening himself against the wall.   "Please don't hurt me. Nice doggie."

Tears cut rivulets through the grime on his cheeks.

The werewolf leapt across the cell and lashed out with razor sharp talons. Michael screamed and clutched at his stomach.   Again it struck, tearing his jerkin and the skin beneath into ribbons.   Under Michael's torn and bleeding hands the tatters of flesh could no longer contain his bowels, which slithered out between his fingers and spilled onto the floor.

"Look at the mess!" Michael muttered, his eyes glazed in shock, "Von Trapp will kill me."

The creature slashed at Michael's throat.   Its nostrils filled with the scent of blood.   Mercifully, Michael was dead before it began to feast upon his flesh.

The Burgomeister continued to listen for some time after the old man's cries had ceased.   He had no desire to inflict unnecessary distress upon anyone, even Michael.   There was a succession of alarming bangs and crashes, then silence. Satisfied that Michael must have found comfort in sleep, he returned to his book.

Chapter 5

Roy Ashton scooped up Ripper's bloody entrails and lowered them carefully into a plastic bucket. Michael Ripper craned his neck to watch. Roy Ashton, a well-built man in his fifties with a shock of prematurely silver hair, handed the bucket to a fresh-faced junior, just two weeks into his apprenticeship.

"Rinse them through with plenty of cold water, dry them thoroughly with towels and a cool hairdryer and dust them lightly with talc," he instructed. His voice was consciously refined, more English than most Englishmen, with barely a hint of the Perth accent of his birth.

The junior nodded earnestly, his excitement in finding himself working at the heart of the British film industry not yet blunted by the mundanity of his duties. The lad trotted off happily. Ashton watched him indulgently, but with a hint of something akin to jealousy.

"You've got to look after them or they perish," He said by way of explanation to Ripper.

"Beg your pardon?" the actor asked.

"The intestines," Ashton explained. "They're made of latex rubber. If you don't protect them from air and sunlight they perish."

He helped the actor sit upright, hitched up what was left of his shirt and set about unfastening the straps that bound the prosthetic stomach appliance to his midriff. Ripper looked down at the flapping strips of bloody, flesh-toned rubber, making no attempt to conceal his distaste.

"Is this what we've been reduced to, Roy?" He asked wearily, "Two and a half thousand years of evolution of the dramatic form and we're spilling rubber guts for the amusement of teenagers? It doesn't feel as if we've moved on from throwing Christians to the lions."

"Well at least the guts *are* rubber these days," replied Ashton, a hint of his antipodean origins surfacing briefly in his inflection. "Anyway, don't knock 'em; those guts are my bread and butter." He freed the prosthetic and lifted it clear of the actor's body.

"Don't get me wrong," said Ripper, rearranging the rags of the shirt as decorously as he could. "I have the greatest respect for your skills. You're as talented a make-up artist as any working today, anywhere. But to what end? Where's the subtlety? The beauty? You, of all people, must feel that."

Ashton had come to England to pursue a career as a professional singer. He was a remarkable man, a true polymath who had originally studied art, music and architecture in Australia. He had been good enough to sing as a principal tenor at Covent Garden, Glyndebourne and even with Benjamin Britten's own English Opera Group, before eventually taking a sideways leap to a more secure career as lead make-up artist at Hammer Films.

He tore a wad of cotton wool from a roll, dampened it with surgical spirit and offered it to Ripper, who set about removing the streaks of theatrical blood from his forearms and stomach before it stained his skin.

Ashton shrugged. "We're just not in the subtlety trade," he said, "It's not what the cinema-going public wants. They're after thrills, gore and sex, and that's what Hammer gives 'em.

"But give us our due, Mick, we do it bloody well. We tell a good story, well-acted, at a cracking pace; and we make a tuppenny-ha'penny production budget look like a million quid."

Ripper couldn't disagree with that. Ashton relieved him of the cotton wool, now crimson with Kensington Gore, the proprietary theatrical blood that looked so shocking when captured on the studio's Eastman Colour film stock, which loved its reds. He dropped it into the rubbish pot in his make-up box.

"Roy, my old cocker, instruct one of your handmaidens to remove my whiskers before I tear the fuckers off myself!"

Ripper & Ashton looked up into the maw of the werewolf. He smiled back at them, revealing bloodstained teeth, and winked a lupine eye.

"Ideally, the one with the big tits," he added.

* * *

Michael Ripper, a gentleman of the old school, was distressed by bad language and couldn't abide vulgarity towards the fairer sex; yet inexplicably forgave Oliver Reed his every transgression, which were manifold. Reed exerted a similar charm upon Ashton and, indeed, on pretty much everybody employed at Bray.

"If you mean Miss Carolgees – and I rather think that you do - she is off with a cold today," said Ashton; "probably because she knew she'd have to fend you off if she wasn't."

"Rot!" said Reed. "She is clearly in love with me. On his deathbed, my dear old father said to me, 'Bob,' he said, for we were on first name terms, 'Never allow yourself to be depilated by an ugly woman, for no good can come of it.' And then he died, peacefully in my arms. Roy, I have upheld that principle religiously in honour his memory and it has served me well. Incidentally, he sends you his regards and suggests that you put your shirt on Strapping Lad in the 3.30 at Chepstow."

"Tell the old reprobate that I no longer have a shirt as a consequence of his last tip."

"I will. In turn, please convey my heartfelt best wishes to the pneumatic Miss Carolgees for a rapid and full recovery, and tell her I am at her service should she need her splendid chest rubbing with Vicks. Failing her, who is the second loveliest flower in your harem?"

"I'm afraid you will have to make do with me," replied Ashton.

"Dear God! I would hate to see any of the flowers below you on the list, no offence. Actually my dear old father added a caveat about avoiding Aussie ponces, but he was delirious and incautious in his use of language, and I wouldn't want to cause any needless offence. Seriously though Roy, the hair is itching like a fucker and the contact lenses are killing me."

"I'm sorry Ollie, let's get you sorted out," said Ashton, rising to his feet, "You don't mind, do you Mike?"

Ripper accepted the offer of Reed's hairy paw and clambered to his feet.

"Of course not," he said, "I've had those full contacts in myself, in She-Devil, and they are murder. I think I'm done for the day, anyway. You're not in make-up again today, are you Oliver?"

"No, thank God," replied Reed, "I've got a bit of business on the Dracula stage in the afternoon if the weather holds, but I don't think I'm wearing anything for that but dried blood and a smile, am I Roy?"

Roy expertly ran a finger around the lids of Reed's left eye. Like a conjuring trick, the contact lens popped out and dropped into his waiting palm. He flipped it over and the eye glared up at him. The iris was yellow, striated and shading to orange at its outer edge, subtly detailed with thread-like red veins.

In shaping the pupil, the maker had abandoned realism for dramatic effect and depicted it as a feline slit. It was a little masterpiece.

"Terry doesn't think we'll get away with your bare arse, so we've decided to keep your trousers on," said Ashton, "But you're definitely not in werewolf make-up; not until you break into the castle."

"I'll see if I can't persuade him to risk it over lunch," replied Reed, "a flash of my naked arse would launch a thousand damp seats in cinemas the world over."

As Ashton took out the second lens, his expression grew serious.

"Don't let him drink too much, Ollie" he said, tipping both into a plastic jar of saline solution and snapping the lid on, "It's starting to make inroads into the production schedule. Lean back and I'll put you some drops in."

Terence Fisher, director of this and of countless other Hammer films, was an alcoholic and currently making little effort to manage his affliction. His lunches at The Crown in the village were extending further and further into the afternoon and when he did return – *if* he did return - he was as often as not incapable of doing his job. Cast and crew were experienced enough to work around him most of the time; but inevitably and increasingly, production time was being lost. The current movie was already running two days behind schedule.

Reed was a boozer himself, a romantic who saw hard drinking as an essential element of the artistic persona. But even he had the discipline to limit his lunchtime drinking to a manageable five or six pints. He accepted a tissue from Ashton and wiped his eyes.

"I'll do what I can," he said, but with no great conviction.

The male cast shared one large changing room with the exception of Christopher Lee and Peter Cushing, whose star status was reflected in named dressing rooms of their own; though neither room was much larger than a wardrobe. Today, Ripper and Reed were the only actors in the common dressing room as they changed for lunch.

Reed stepped out of the shower, as unmindful of his nakedness as only the exceptionally beautiful can be. He was holding a plug of hair that he had rescued from the plughole; some sodden strands of the werewolf pelt that Ashton had missed when cleaning him up.

"Yak," he said, dropping it into the waste basket.

"I beg your pardon?" asked Ripper, buttoning his shirt. He had foregone the shower in favour of a bath when he got home and was almost dressed.

"It's Yak hair, apparently. Roy says it shows up better on camera."

Reed picked up his towel and rubbed himself down vigorously.

"Really? Well isn't that a wonderful thing?" said Ripper, then paused. His own phrase had triggered some shadowy memory within him. After a moment's introspection he spoke again.

"Have you ever dreamed that you were in a film or a play, Oliver?" He asked. Reed considered the question.

"I have endless anxiety dreams," he replied, "all the classic ones everyone has: I'm on stage and I've forgotten all my lines, or I'm suddenly aware that I'm starkers. Is that the kind of thing you mean?"

"Not really. I mean actually *in* a film. Not acting, but being part of it."

"I don't understand," said Reed, throwing his towel onto the bench and fishing his y-fronts out of his locker.

Ripper had walked over to the hand basin and was adjusting his tie in the mirror.

"I had this dream recently," he said over his shoulder. "Well, I say I did: but to be honest, I can't even remember when or if I did dream it. I just have a vague memory of believing that I was a character in a film. A Hammer film."

"When you say being a character, you don't mean being *in* character: you mean actually being *a* character?" asked Reed, pulling on his jeans. "Bugger me Mike! That's a bit metaphysical, isn't it? Have you been at the Pirandello again?"

Ripper smiled at the young actor's reflection in the mirror.

"I don't think I was aware that I was fictional," he said. "I'm not sure I aware of much at all. I don't think I was the most self-aware of characters."

"No, I can honestly say I've never had anything remotely like that," Reed replied, "I hope you were being paid overtime."

Ripper chuckled.

"I don't think so. Or if I did, it was just in dream money."

He reached into his locker and lifted his overcoat off the hook.

Reed had caught up with him and swung his leather bomber over his shoulder.

"Did it bother you?"

Ripper shrugged.

"Not really," he replied, "though it makes me wonder whether I've been in one Hammer shocker too many."

"One Hammer film is one too many, Mike, but they pay the bills. The smaller bills, anyway. Time for a pint before you head off?"

Ripper weighed the relative attractions of an early bath and lunch at The Crown.

"Go on," he said, "just the one."

* * *

By the time they reached the pub, Terence Fisher was already ensconced in his favourite seat by the fire, with a drink in one hand, a cigarette in the other and two tumblers, empty but for slices of lemon and melting ice, on the table in front of him.

He raised his glass in salute.

"Another, Terry?" asked Reed as he made his way to the bar.

"Large gin and tonic if you're offering, old boy," Fisher replied.

"Mike?"

"I'll have a pint of stout, please," Ripper replied, positioning himself at the bar so that Reed stood between him and Fisher.

"Remember what Roy said about Terry's drinking," he murmured quietly.

"Roy's an old woman!" scoffed Reed. "I'll make sure he gets back in one piece."

When the landlord had given him his change, Reed expertly gathered together Fisher's drink and his own pint of bitter and whiskey chaser, and made his way over to the fire. Ripper followed behind with his pint.

"An excellent death, Mike," said Fisher when the two had joined him, "One of your best, I think."

Ripper accepted the compliment with a noncommittal nod.

"Certainly one of the goriest," he replied.

"Michael is troubled," said Oliver.

"How so?" asked Fisher.

"He's been working overtime without pay."

Fisher glanced across at Ripper with genuine concern. Ripper smiled.

"Only in my sleep Terry," He explained. "I had a sort of dream that I was a character in a Hammer film."

Fisher continued to observe Ripper through his heavy rimmed spectacles, flicked the ash off his cigarette and took a drag. He smiled.

"That would be a matter for Equity," he said, blowing out smoke. "There again, perhaps it wouldn't; I think you only get paid for *playing* a role. *Being* a character is in your own time. Who were you?"

"It was just a character role," Ripper replied. "I wouldn't have minded if it had been Hamlet -"

"- I bloody would!" interrupted Reed, "Hamlet has a rotten time of it, poor bastard, and he's riddled with angst to boot. No, if I was going to be a fictional character I'd choose one who has a bit of fun. Dom Juan perhaps, or Tom Jones. Or what about James Bond? I'd get to bed all those dolly birds, shoot the bad guys and drive around in a Bentley Continental."

"I think you'd make an excellent James Bond," observed Fisher, "Better than that Scottish roughneck they've cast for *Doctor No*."

Reed raised his pint in thanks for the compliment.

"Well, I was nothing so grand or so debauched," continued Ripper, determined to get his story out, "Just an amalgamation of characters I've played in other Hammer shockers. You know: a derelict drunkard whose only purpose in the plot is to provide an early victim for the monster."

"And *were* you a victim of the monster?" asked Fisher.

"I was, Terry, more than once. And because I was a real character, I was really killed. It hurt!"

They continued to chat for a few minutes on the existential consequences of discovering that one was fictional. Fisher's gin disappeared in short order, and when he rose to get another round in, Ripper made his apologies and left, not wanting to conspire in what seemed likely to descend into an all-afternoon drinking session.

Fisher returned from the bar carrying a tray.

"Now, Terry, about my arse," said Oliver.

Chapter 6

A black speck winged its way slowly across the starry ceiling of the night. In the east the sky had only just started to brighten, but the raven could already distinguish every detail of the valley below. From its high vantage point, its sharp eyes scanned the length and breadth of the vale of Walach in its quest for the first meal of the day.

Spying no easy pickings on the steaming ash-heaps of the village, it wheeled about to scour Hob Crag for carrion. It followed the slope of the hill, ascending until it rose above the black towers of Castle Dracula. Beyond the castle, a sheer cliff dropped giddily towards the leafy treetops of Karnstein forest far below. The raven circled the battlements. It had eaten well here before. This morning, however, the courtyard was empty and the doors and windows all barred. It was about to fly on when it spotted something on the drawbridge.

It began a long descent, spiralling towards the ground and landing at a safe distance atop a stone finial surmounting one of the gate posts. From the safety of this perch, carved, as chance would have it, in grotesque mockery of its own form, it studied its find.

The body lay face down, naked but for a pair of tattered breeches. Its bare feet were scratched and bruised, its fingernails ragged and torn. Of more interest to the raven, however, was the blood caked on its body and clotting in its hair. It hopped down onto the balustrade and from there to the weather-beaten planking, from whence it began cautiously to approach the body. It only a foot or two away when the figure moaned and rolled over. With a startled squawk the raven took back to the air.

Talbot awoke with the taste of blood in his mouth and knew that the madness had been upon him again. He hoped that the blood was that of some animal, but knew from bitter experience that it was probably not. His gorge rose and he staggered to his feet, managing to find the drawbridge rail just in time to spew black vomit into the moat. He wiped his mouth, and then buried his face in his hands. Anguished sobs racked his body, and tears dissolved the brown stains on his face and hands, bringing them back to crimson life. When the edge of his pain had been dulled, he tried to recall the events that had brought him to the god-forsaken place.

He remembered coming upon the smelly peasant in the forest, and their subsequent disastrous cart ride. He hoped sincerely that it was not Michael's blood on his hands; for in the short time he had known him he had developed a perverse liking for the old man. He remembered also the priest, Father Shandor, giving him the terrible news about Constance; his arrest and subsequent confinement at the hands of the Burgomeister. Beyond that his memory was blank. It was always the same after one of his attacks.

Abandoning any hope of retrieving the last few hours he took stock of the present.

Across the drawbridge, a massive portcullis barred the way. A shiver ran down his spine as he read the name above. Now he understood what had brought him here. He knew from past horrors that when the fit was upon him he was able to follow a victim's scent as easily as a beast of prey. It seemed to him that this time, while he had been in the grip of his curse, some lingering spark of his normal self had harnessed the beast to guide him to his fiancé. Once again, destiny had played its perverse hand.

Before going any further he had to wash away the terrible legacy of his madness. He walked off the drawbridge and clambered down the steep bank to the moat. The water was foul and stagnant. Unperturbed, he scrubbed at his face and chest. A scarlet flower bloomed across the water. He was rinsing out his hair when a loud mechanical clangour made him look up. The chains were being wound in, swaying and snapping as the tension increased. The drawbridge started to lift.

He scrambled back up the bank, his wet feet slipping and sliding on the muddy slope. The drawbridge was already above head height and rising. It had to be now or never. He ran full-tilt along the path, hurled himself from the edge of the moat and caught the lip of the drawbridge with the fingertips of one hand. He swung wildly, twisting in mid-air to get a better grip. The drawbridge carried him up until it slammed against the castle wall with an impact that threatened to dislodge him and send him hurtling down into the moat.

Talbot swung a leg over the edge of the drawbridge and clambered astride it. Prior to jumping he had not had time to consider his course of action from here. He looked up. Above him rose a sheer wall without ledges or sills, pierced only by the thin slits of windows.

A few feet to either side of the gothic archway, however, the gargoyles that decorated the buttresses might just provide the hand and foot holds he needed to reach the battlements. He edged along to the end of the drawbridge, and then carefully rose until he was crouched upon the edge. His heart pounded furiously; he took a deep breath and leapt into space.

* * *

Under cover of the dark, a sinister figure crept through the village and stopped outside the gates of Bumblewicz' workshop. With a quick glance up and down the empty street it opened one of the gates and slipped through. It flitted across the deserted courtyard like a moon-shadow, and let itself into the potting shed. Once it had shut the door, it stood a lantern on the refectory table and opened the shutters. Light flooded the room and illuminated the trespasser's features.

Although still a young man, his face was already deeply lined, and his lank black hair streaked with grey. His nose was hooked, his eyes dark and glittering. It could have been the face of a doctor, or even a priest, but it was not. He was a grave-robber, and his name was Klove.

He had been born in Karnstein, the son of a whore. His mother, Elsbieta, was a plain, strong woman who had worked in The Lair for most of her adult life. Although Klove had not been planned, Elsbieta had been delighted with her child and had proven to be a devoted and loving mother.

The Lair of the White Worm, to give it its full name, was Karnstein's brothel, named after a monstrous serpent of ancient legend. At least, so claimed Nellie Bowlegs, its founder and proprietress: though her clientele occasionally wondered whether it might not have a more cynical origin than that.

Klove's early memories were of an idyllic childhood spent in the warmth and security of the bawdy house. When Elsbieta was called upstairs he could take his pick from half a dozen well-upholstered and perfumed bosoms in which to nestle. The clients, by-and-large, treated him with the affection of benevolent uncles, for none of them could be sure that he was not their own bastard son. They would regularly bring him treats, or slip him a penny before they crept home to their families. If Elsbieta was aware of the identity of the true father, then she chose to keep it to herself.

As he had grown into youth, the women had pooled their skills to teach Klove how to read and write. Nellie taught him the rudiments of arithmetic and accounting, and he had approached manhood with the promise of a bright future.

On the eve of his sixteenth birthday, however, Elsbieta had called him to her room and spoken to him alone. A few minutes later the young man's howls of grief and rage had shaken the building; then he had burst out of the room, tumbled down the stairs and disappeared into the night.

Nobody knew what terrible crime or secret shame Elsbieta had confessed to her son that night. Amongst the villagers there was speculation that the two of them had committed a crime against nature so hideous that it should not be whispered about, although they had managed to for a while. The other whores who worked at the Lair had known better, but had kept their own counsel. Elsbieta had never spoken of the incident, and before long it had faded into obscurity, whilst she had continued to satisfy the desires of the town's menfolk, if not their curiosity.

After wandering the rain-washed slopes of the mountainside all night, Klove had collapsed. There he had lain without food or water through the following day and night. By all rights he should have died there.

In fact, when he awoke he had found himself in a warm room, lying on a cot and covered with a blanket. On a table beside the bed was a bowl of broth and some bread and, hanging over the chair, a dry set of clothes. He had not the faintest idea where he was, or how he had got there.

When he had eaten and dressed a knock came at the door, and a distinguished figure had entered. He was tall and gaunt, with dark hair greying at the temples. He wore the apparel of a gentleman, and carried a doctor's bag.

"Good morning, young man," he had said. "I trust you slept well?"

"Wonderful well, thank you sir," Klove had replied. "But, begging your pardon, sir, may I ask your name and where I might be? For if it was you or your men what rescued me from the mountainside, then I reckon I owes you my life."

"Time enough for questions when you are fully recovered," the gentleman had said, opening his bag and taking out a bottle. He had poured a treacly liquid into a spoon.

"What you need at the moment is rest. Drink this," Klove had obediently swallowed the bitter medicine. The gentleman closed his bag and picked it up.

"Stay here for now," he had said. "I will bring you some luncheon at mid-day. I keep no staff, but if you need anything just call. I will hear you. My name is Frankenstein. Baron Frankenstein."

Klove had slept through the morning, and only awoken when the Baron returned with food and more medicine. Over luncheon he had learned that the Baron was indeed a doctor, and that he lived alone in the castle he had inherited at birth. The solitude suited him, however, for he was engaged in medical research that he could pursue uninterrupted in his lonely retreat. He explained how he had discovered the young man on the mountainside, soaked to the skin and delirious with fever, and half-carried, half-dragged him back to the Castle.

On the Baron's suggestion Klove had stayed at the castle that night and the following day, regaining his strength and enjoying the dreamy slumber induced by the medicine. The day had stretched into another, and the days into a week. As he recovered, he began to take on domestic duties around the castle, and to ever more eagerly anticipate the euphoria following his daily medication.

The Baron had observed the development of his addiction with more than clinical interest, for it was a necessary part of the plan he had devised when first he clapped eyes on the lad. As the weeks progressed he had gradually increased the dose until Laudanum was no longer sufficient to satisfy Klove's craving. Then he had introduced the needle.

Before long he had in the young man a loyal slave, more than willing to relieve him of the mundane chores which distracted him from his experiments. Furthermore, it took only the threat of withholding of Klove's morphine to persuade him to take on additional unsavoury duties, such as robbing graves.

When times were slack, the Baron sometimes allowed Klove to use his telescope. The lad would train it down the valley and spend hours watching the villagers going about their daily business. Occasionally he would catch a glimpse of his mother. Today, however, he had witnessed the dramatic appearance of the carter and had looked on with growing excitement at the subsequent gory slapstick as the corpse was un-skewered from the cart shaft. When it had been deposited in the potting shed he had hurried off to inform his master of the fresh arrival.

Since the Chapel of Rest had last been broken into, Dame Bumblewicz had sewn the corpse into a burlap sack, ready for its burial the following day. The only other concession she had made to the dignity of the departed was to plug the wound in its stomach with Michael's discarded breeches. What more could anyone expect for the pittance the state would pay, via the Burgomeister, for a pauper's funeral?

Klove was not arguing: they had saved him the job of prising off a coffin lid. He lifted the sack onto his shoulder as easily as if it were a bundle of rags, closed the lantern doors and carried the load out into the night.

* * *

Elsewhere in the village, Father Shandor was lying awake in his bed. He had slept fitfully for an hour or two, but bad dreams had finally woken him shortly after midnight and he had not been able to get back to sleep since.

There was plenty to occupy his thoughts. So many evil omens in such a short period. They were massing together like carrion birds above an ailing steer, waiting for the moment to swoop.

First, there had been the death of Philomena Blepp. Sadly, that had been nothing out of the ordinary in itself: but considered alongside the events that had followed, it had taken on dark significance.

Then there was the matter of the four strangers. In Shandor's experience, when strangers came to Karnstein, trouble was never far behind. This party had proven no exception. Their very presence had seemed to awaken Karnstein's twins of evil; the two castles, Frankenstein and Dracula. Their prattle had implied that the former was once more in occupation, and they had disappeared into the latter under mysterious and disturbing circumstances.

The bizarre death of the carter had seemed to have a natural explanation, but even there, questions remained unanswered. What was the identity of the mysterious figure who, if Michael's account could be believed, had been responsible for the accident?

Shandor cocked an ear. Curious: he could hear somebody moving down in the churchyard. He slipped out of bed and crept across to the window. Down in the west corner of the graveyard a light was flickering.

Shandor dressed in the dark and hurried downstairs. He collected his hunting rifle from the cupboard in his study, slipped out of the front door and crept through the churchyard, using the trees for cover. As he approached the light he could make out hushed voices and the indistinct sound of labour.

When he was near enough he took up position behind an ivy-covered gravestone. Light from a partially shuttered lantern on the grass threw its beam across the freshly dug grave of poor Philomena Blepp. Around the grave stood three of Shandor's most upright parishioners; Hans Muller, Yeoman Woblinz and John the Smith. Muller and the woodcutter leant on spades while Smith rummaged in a burlap sack. All around them was heaped up the very soil that Mole had thrown upon Miss Blepp's coffin less than two days ago.

As Shandor looked on in bewilderment and with a growing sense of outrage, another shovelful of soil was thrown out of the black cavity of the grave to add to the heap of spoil. A moment later there was a hollow thud and a voice from the grave hissed,

"I've reached the bottom! Chuck down the ropes."

Smith pulled a couple of ropes out of the sack and threw them down into the hole. Muted oaths drifted up from the open grave. One by one, the ends of each rope were flicked up onto the mounds of dirt. Then the voice called again.

"Get me out of here!"

Muller stabbed the blade of his spade into the heap of soil and reached down into the grave. Shandor eyes widened as Mole himself clambered out of the pit.

"Dig it out, fill it in, dig it out again," he grumbled, flinging down his shovel, "I tell you this; you lot can fill the bastard back in."

Smith reassured him in an undertone that the other members of the party would replace the soil, then allocated an end of a rope to each. Slowly and laboriously they hauled the coffin out of the grave. When it was clear of the hole, they lowered it onto the grass. Muller swept the dirt off the lid with his sleeve.

Smith produced a nail bar from the sack, bent over the casket and dug it under the lid. The nails squealed in protest as he pushed down, and the lid lifted an inch. Smith threw down the jemmy and finished the job with his hands, throwing the lid onto the heap of spoil.

From his vantage point, Shandor could see the corpse of Philomena Blepp, eerily illuminated by the flickering light of the lantern. She lay in the coffin with her hands folded neatly in her lap, her skin ivory white against the bottle green of her Sunday dress.

The four men stood transfixed, looking down into the open coffin. Woblinz crossed himself.

"Hurry up John!" urged Mole. "I don't like this one bloody bit."

Smith emptied the last two items out of the sack; a small lump-hammer and a length of wood. One end of the billet had been sharpened.

Smith knelt beside the coffin and rested the point of the stake on the corpse's breast. As he raised the hammer, Shandor could take no more. He rose to his full impressive height and stepped out from the shadow of the gravestone.

"Blasphemers!" he roared.

The four men leapt into the air simultaneously.

"What in God's name do you think you are doing?" He bellowed.

Shandor glowered at them from under bristling eyebrows. There was no reply. He turned his attention to the gravedigger.

"Mole! You, of all people! What is your explanation for this sacrilege?"

Unable to return Shandor's unwavering stare, Mole stared at his feet and said nothing.

Finally, Smith found his voice.

"It has to be done, Father," he muttered.

"What has to be done, John?"

Smith swallowed nervously and held up the stake and hammer.

"The corpse must be pierced through the heart, that the soul may be set free."

A succession of expressions flickered across Shandor's face: bewilderment, disbelief and finally outrage. He strode across to Smith, tore the tools from his hands and flung them to the ground.

"Get out! All of you!" he shouted, pushing Smith away in disgust.

"Look out!" cried Muller.

Something landed with massive impact on Shandor's back and clung on, sending him reeling towards the other men.

Smith leapt forwards and grabbed Philomena's hair just in time to prevent her from sinking razor-sharp incisors into the priest's neck. Shandor heard the snap of her jaws a fraction of an inch from his ear.

Blepp screamed in animal rage and leapt from Shandor's back with the agility and strength of an ape, twisting in mid-air to land on Smith, who fell to the ground with the creature on top of him.

"The stake!" shouted Smith. He was fighting a losing battle against the girl, clutching her throat with one hand, and fending off her attempts to scratch out his eyes with the other.

Shandor stood rooted to the spot. Woblinz rushed forward, picked up the stake and with both hands thrust it into Philomena's back.

She screaming hideously and rolled off Smith onto the heap of spoil, reaching behind her back with both hands, desperately trying to pull out the stake. Smith sat up and pointed a trembling finger at her.

"It's not pierced her heart! It must be driven in deeper!"

At last Shandor found the will to move. He stepped up behind the girl and with a well-aimed kick drove the stake right through her back. The tip burst through her breast in a spurt of blood, and then she was still.

Smith staggered to his feet and wiped the blood from his face.

"Can you doubt now that He has returned?" he asked Shandor.

Although his every limb was trembling with a shock that was only going to grow, the Father picked up a spade.

"Come," he muttered, "let us rebury poor Philomena; then we must talk."

Chapter 7

The Burgomeister was having trouble with his last mushroom. He pursued it around the plate with his fork before cornering it in the cleavage of his chop-bone. With an air of triumph he impaled it and popped it into his mouth.

"He seems such a nice young man," Dame von Trapp said.

She was trying to persuade her husband to free Talbot, in whom she had developed a more than compassionate interest.

"You could find him work around the farm. The men would be able to keep an eye on him. He's educated too; perhaps he could help with your correspondence."

In truth, the Burgomeister needed little persuasion to release the stranger. His only concern had been the possibility that Talbot might abuse his freedom by heading for the castle in pursuit of his fiancé and her companions. His wife's suggestion addressed that problem. He wiped his mouth on his sleeve.

"Now now, little woman," he admonished indulgently, "It is not your place to interfere in my judicial responsibilities. As it happens, it was my intention to release Herr Talbot on parole into my own supervision anyway."

Piss off, little man, his wife thought silently, clearing away the plates.

When his breakfast had settled Von Trapp took the keys from the hook beside the front door and walked across the courtyard. Overhead, the first glimmerings of dawn stained the sky blood-red. Shepherd's warning, he thought. As he neared the cell outbuilding he was surprised to see that the door was wide open. He tried to recall whether he had latched it the previous evening. If it had been ajar all night his prisoners would have had a draughty time of it. No wonder Michael had been squawking.

His initial surprise was as nothing to the seismic shock which overcame him as it gradually dawned on him that the door was not merely open, but actually lying about him in splinters on the ground.

"What in thunder?" he bellowed, rushing into the building. He gazed around in horror. The interrogation room looked as if it had been hit by a bomb. The desk had been overturned and the chair hurled against the wall. The cupboard doors were hanging off and the shelves had been ransacked. Worse than any of this, however, was the sight of the cell door, which had been torn from its hinges and lay twisted on the floor.

The Burgomeister staggered to the doorway and clutched the lintel for support. The floor was strewn with pot shards, straw, and coagulating puddles of what looked suspiciously like blood. The cot frames were twisted beyond recognition. Von Trapp clambered over the grisly remains of one of the mattresses.

"Gerroff! Fuggibastod!" came a stifled voice under his feet.

The Burgomeister threw the mattress aside. Underneath, Michael lay curled amid the debris. He yawned and sat up.

"Is it time for breakfast?" he asked, then looked around the cell. "Bugger me!" He exclaimed. "What's gone off here then?"

"Some bastard has destroyed my jail, that's what!" Von Trapp grabbed Michael by the hair and started to shake him.

"Was it you?" he screamed, "because if it was, I swear to God I'll cut off your ballocks and feed them to the pigs."

Put like this, the question was hardly likely to elicit a positive response, even from someone as dim as Michael.

"I-I n-never!" he squeaked.

76

"Who was it, then? Tell me!"

Michael hadn't a clue. His recollection of the events of the preceding evening did not stretch beyond the Burgomeister's interview with Talbot. He was well aware that this would not satisfy Von Trapp, so he improvised hastily.

"It was that Herr Talbot, Burgomeister. He had one of his loony turns," he said, unaware just how close his invention came to the truth.

"I tried to stop him, but he was as strong as ten oxes. I was lucky to escape with my life."

The Burgomeister let go of Michael's hair and wiped his hand on his breeches. He gazed desolately at the ruins of his pride and joy.

"The man is obviously a danger to the public," he said, "he must be recaptured immediately, dead or alive."

* * *

Michael sat alone on the cell floor. Outside, he could hear the Burgomeister shouting orders to his hastily mustered search party. A draught blew through the building. Michael shivered and pulled the tattered remnants of his shirt together.

Overnight, several angry red weals had appeared upon his belly and chest, adding to the patchwork of scar tissue which already covered his torso. He was not much concerned by this new disfigurement: for as long as he could remember he had been covered with scars. Some had faded over many years; others were livid and recent. Every few weeks he would wake to discover a new addition. He was never able to remember a single detail of the events of the evenings preceding the appearance of these mysterious stigmata, and it had never occurred to him to wonder how or why they appeared. He had always assumed that the same thing happened to everyone, and had not thought the subject worthy of discussion. It was just one of those things.

He was as much in the dark about how his shirt had come to be shredded upon his back. Crumpled in a corner, however, was a snowy white garment he recognised as Herr Talbot's chemise. Perhaps Talbot had gone barmy after all, he thought. He hoped not, for despite their short acquaintance he liked the young master. He was ready with his purse too, and soft touches were a rare commodity in Karnstein.

He held the chemise up in front of him. It was cut from fine silk, with puffed sleeves and pearl buttons; a bit camp for his own tastes, but he was in no position to be fussy. Doubts still lingered in his mind about Talbot's sexual orientation, and the young man's flamboyant taste in clothes only served to fuel his suspicions. He vaguely remembered Talbot also mentioning something about unnatural acts with animals, but Michael was inclined to be more indulgent about that, for personal reasons. He stripped off what was left of his old shirt and clambered into the chemise.

Decently clad, he clambered over the rubble to the empty doorway and cocked an ear. In his rage, Von Trapp had forgotten to give Michael any instructions before he had stormed out. Whilst he was sure that the Burgomeister was too humane a man to expect him to continue to serve out his custodial sentence in the wrecked cell, he did not intend to consult with him on the point, just in case he was wrong.

Michael heard Von Trapp give the order to ride out. He waited until the clatter of the horses' hooves had died away before he stepped out into the interrogation room. In order to ensure that the party was well on its way before he left, he spent another minute kicking through the rubbish on the floor.

Under one of the upturned drawers he discovered the loaf of bread that Talbot had kicked across the room last night. As he bent down to pick it up he experienced a momentary terrifying *deja vu*. He paused for a moment with the loaf halfway to his mouth, then shrugged and bit into it.

"Did the stranger wreak all this destruction himself?"

Michael looked up from his feast. The Burgomeister's wife stood in the doorway surveying the damage. She turned a disdainful eye upon Michael. Dame Von Trapp was not over-fond of him, having never forgiven him for something he had once shown her in the woods.

"'Fraid so, Ma'am," he replied.

"He must have been like an animal," she observed, moistening her lips. "Did he get away?"

"He's got a few hours on the search party, Ma'am, but if anyone can track him down I'm sure that the Burgomeister will."

"I doubt it," she replied. "Was he angry?"

"Steaming, Ma'am, and effing fit to burst a blood vessel."

"Oh good," she said absently, and turned to leave.

Michael breathed a sigh of relief. He breathed too soon. Dame von Trapp's head appeared around the doorway again.

"What do you think you are doing here anyway, you foul ape?" she snapped, "creeping around our property. Piss off! Go on, shoo!"

Never one to inspect a gift horse at all, let alone too closely, Michael mumbled his apologies and fled.

As soon as he had rounded the first corner and was out of view of the Manor he slackened his pace, and before long had to stop altogether. He stood in the middle of the road, gasping for breath, with perspiration streaming down his face. His was not a body designed for exercise. In point of fact, it was hard to imagine just what it had been designed for. Drinking, maybe.

As soon as he had got his wind back, he continued at a gentler pace. As he walked, he weighed up the pros and cons of his present situation. On the one hand, he was a free man, decked out from head to toe in new-found clothes, and heading towards the village on a sunny morning. On the other, he was broke and he could not ignore the possibility that there might be unpleasantness when he next bumped into either the Burgomeister or Bumblewicz. On the positive side once again, he knew that a crate which had been bound for Dr. Pretorius now lay submerged beneath the murky waters of the Farkle. Surely, he thought, he should be able to extract some money from the Doctor in exchange for that information. Skirting around the village, he headed out along the long and winding Abbey Road.

Karnstein Abbey was a ruin straight out of a gothic novel. Its broken arches and crumbling buttresses hinted at the grandeur of its past. In its time it had been the spiritual and intellectual centre of the Vale of Walach: but the reforming zeal of the Brethren had put paid to that. They had burnt down the library, shattered the stained glass and hung the monks from the vaults, all in the name of God, who had looked on and chosen, with lofty restraint, not to intervene on behalf of one side or the other of the unpleasantness. As the centuries passed, successive generations of villagers had driven out here under cover of the night to steal the carved masonry for their barns and pigsties. Now ivy protected what remained of the walls, and moss covered the ancient tombstones. The place gave Michael the willies.

The Dormitorium had worn the passing years better than the rest of the Abbey, a fact that had not escaped the enigmatic Dr. Pretorius when he had first appeared in the village. After courting both the Burgomeister and Father Shandor with calculated charm, he had set about converting it to suit his needs with their joint blessing – a rare achievement. He built living accommodation for himself and his staff, and fitted out a laboratory with retorts, furnaces and, for decoration, an array of biological curiosities pickled in bottles. Behind its stout doors he was able to resume the hermetic research for which he had been expelled from Prague.

Michael pulled the handle set into in the wall, and heard the distant tinkle of the bell within. Before long there came the tread of approaching feet, stopping short the other side of the door. A key grated in the lock, several bolts shot noisily and eventually the door swung slowly inwards. Michael looked up nervously at the massive ebony-skinned figure of Joachim, Pretorius' mute manservant.

"I - WANT - TO - SPEAK - WITH - YOUR - MASTER," he bellowed, as if speaking to an idiot child, and pointed into the house. Joachim eyed him with undisguised loathing, then turned and disappeared back into the gloom. Michael waited.

As the minutes wore on he started to fidget. He began to kick idly at the boot-scraper. By the time Joachim reappeared he had wedged his boot fast under it. Joachim beckoned for Michael to follow him and headed back down the hall. Afraid that he might miss his chance Michael wrenched his foot out of the boot and followed.

As he caught up with the manservant, Pretorius emerged from his bedroom, tying the cord of his dressing gown. He was not a tall man, but made it up by being so painfully thin that he managed to look spindly all the same. In compensation for the shiny dome of his crown he grew his snow-white hair long at the back and sides. He had bad breath, an acerbic temperament and frequently, as on this occasion, a hangover.

"This had better be bloody good," he snarled, directing Michael into the study, "because if it's not I shall take pleasure in asking Joachim to rip off your ears."

Michael stood in the middle of the carpet, wringing his hands and shooting nervous glances at Joachim.

"I didn't mean for the savage to wake you up, Herr Doctor," he whined. Pretorius sighed impatiently.

"You had better leave, Joachim, or I will get no sense out of this babbling fool. Perhaps you could ask Dominique to mix me one of her specials. I am somewhat incommoded."

The manservant gave Michael another baleful stare and left, silently closing the doors behind him. Pretorius let himself down gently into a chair.

"Now stop squirming and tell me what you have to say."

Michael plan had been to tease Pretorius with hints and suggestions, working him into a frenzy of frustrated acquisitiveness until he was in a position to extract a tidy sum for information leading to the recovery of the box. Fear acted as a verbal enema, however, and his words gushed out uncontrollably.

"There's a crate fallen in the river what was being delivered to you but there was an accident and it fell in. It come all the way from Eejit."

Pretorius sat up and took interest.

"Egypt?"

"That's the town, Herr Doctor."

"And you say it fell in the river? Could you show me where?"

"I could try. Perhaps if there was some reyumenation - "

"Yes, yes," Pretorius muttered impatiently. He pulled a bell-rope and a few moments later Joachim reappeared, bearing a tray upon which was a glass containing a dirty brown liquid. The doctor snatched it up and drained it in one, then shuddered.

"Fetch ropes and a grappling hook, Joachim, and harness the trap. We are going fishing."

* * *

"It was here, I swear," whined Michael.

"Shut up!" replied Pretorius impatiently. "I'm well aware that you don't have the wit to invent such a tale. Joachim, try a little further along the bank. Perhaps the current has driven it downstream."

Joachim hauled in the grappling hook and shot a filthy look at Michael. He had been at it for half an hour now, hurling the hook into the river over and over again on the peasant's instructions, and had so far dredged up nothing but a long abandoned wicker basket and a great deal of foul smelling weed. He was beginning to suspect that the whole thing was a hoax perpetrated by Michael simply to humiliate him. If it was, the peasant would pay. He walked a few yards down river, looped the rope and tried again.

Pretorius shouted instructions from the top of the bank, dressed in the customary tight black clothes that gave him the appearance of a superannuated spider. Michael limped up and down the bank anxiously. He had been obliged to leave his boot under Pretorius' scraper, and his filthy hose was now holed and dew-sodden. Joachim threw another handful of weed on the heap.

"Tell me about the accident again, worm," said Pretorius. Michael stopped pacing and recounted the story of the cart ride. When he got to the part about the strangely dressed foreigner whose dramatic appearance in the road had frightened the horses, Pretorius interrupted.

"You say he wore a hat?"

Michael looked embarrassed, "not a hat, Herr Doctor, a flowerpot."

"As you wish. It was red, then?"

"Yes."

"With sloping sides?"

"Yup."

"And it was flat on top?"

"That's right, Herr Doctor, an ordinary flowerpot."

"A fez!" Pretorius exclaimed, making the already nervous Michael jump. "I thought so!"

At that moment Joachim started waving to attract Pretorius' attention and uttering the grunts which were the only sounds his mutilated mouth was able to make. Pretorius clambered to his feet.

"Have you found it? Well done! Don't just stand there, Michael, help him!"

Michael hobbled down the bank and tried to look useful as Joachim hauled the rope in. Pretorius joined them at the river's edge and milled about excitedly.

A corner of the crate broke the surface. Joachim waded into the river and with awesome strength pulled it up onto the bank. Somehow the lid had been lost in the river, and the open crate had filled with water. It poured out through the joints and knot-holes, emptying slowly to reveal a coffin-like box hewn from alabaster. As the level of the water fell, so did Pretorius' face. He plunged his arms into the water and began to feel around inside the box frantically.

84

"It's gone!" he exclaimed. "The sarcophagus is empty! Hell and damnation!"

He lashed out at the crate, turned and stormed back up the bank.

"This is the work of Turhan Bey!" he muttered.

* * *

In an isolated peat-cutter's cottage not far from Karnstein, Turhan Bey was drying out the mummy of Kharis, High Priest of the Temple of Osiris. He fussed around the hearth like a mother hen, stirring the embers in the grate and keeping an eye out for stray sparks. Steam rising from the damp bandages filled the room with the odour of strange spices and putrefaction.

Bey was a thousand miles from home, and looked it. Apart from the fez he wore a grey djeballa and sported a neat moustache that he had grown in an attempt to lend an air of maturity to his round and youthful face. Around his neck he wore the Sacred Ankh: for Turhan Bey, too, was a High Priest, linked to Kharis in an unbroken line of worship which reached back into the mists of time.

In his native land, he had been responsible for protecting the secrecy of the ancient sites. Somehow the location of one of these, the tomb of Princess Ananka, had fallen into the hands of an infidel lord from across the sea. Ananka, the living Goddess, who had died at the height of her legendary beauty, two thousand years before the birth of Christ.

Legend told how, driven mad with grief, her lover, the High Priest Kharis had attempted the ultimate heresy. Returning to her tomb secretly, he had embarked on the ritual which would bring her back to life, or at least a semblance of it; the reading of the Scroll of Thoth. Before he had completed the ritual he was discovered. In punishment for his crime he had been mummified alive and entombed with the Princess in order to protect her final resting-place from desecration forever. He had not done a very good job of it.

When the English lord had started to dig in the Valley of the Kings, Bey had joined the party as interpreter. In this position he was able both to keep an eye on their progress and also to subtly interfere with it. Eventually the infidel had found him out in his sabotage, and had thrown him off the site. Shortly afterwards the Englishman had broken into the tomb and defiled the sleep of Princess Ananka.

Bey had made sure that the infidel paid for his crime, but not before the contents of the tomb had been taken to Cairo and sold like cheap souvenirs. Kharis' mummy had passed through various hands until finally Dr. Pretorius had bought it for his researches. Bey, had pursued it relentlessly out of Africa and across Europe, finally catching up with it yesterday at Farkle Bridge.

He had returned to the river that same night to retrieve the mummy. As an orphan child growing up in Port Said he had survived by diving for coins thrown overboard by travellers and sailors coming in to dock. Negotiating the icy waters of the Farkle by night had proven an altogether more challenging task. With the protection of the trusty Hippopotamus Goddess Tawaret, however, and a liberal application of hog's lard, he had managed to find the crate, jemmy the lid and rescue Kharis.

Bey stepped over the corpse of the peat cutter and went through to the bedroom. It was set out as a rudimentary temple to Osiris. The walls were hung with papyrus images, and jackal-faced idols stood either side of the draped bed that served as an altar. Nearby, hanging over a small brazier, an infusion of sacred Tana leaves simmered in a bronze cauldron. On the altar stood the elaborately decorated tabernacle containing the blasphemous Scroll of Thoth.

These were the instruments Bey needed to wake Kharis from his sleep. In five nights' time, when the Dog Star was in fortuitous alignment, he would repeat that ritual for which his predecessor had paid so terrible a price. Now, the Scroll of Thoth would restore Kharis to a twilight life for long enough to take his revenge.

Bey sniffed the air. Something was burning. With an Egyptian epithet he dashed back into the front room, tripped over the peat-cutter's legs and went flying. He picked himself up and limped over to the fireplace. Wisps of acrid smoke mingled with the steam above the hearth. He rolled the mummy over and inspected it for damage. The bandages had scorched all the way down its right side. He snuffed out a smouldering thread between finger and thumb.

"For this and for all the other indignities you have suffered, the infidel Doctor will pay with his life," he hissed.

Chapter 8

Talbot dragged himself over the battlements of Castle Dracula and collapsed, exhausted, onto the parapet. He gazed up at the bright morning sky, enjoying the coldness of the stone flags against his back.

He still had no clear plan of what he was going to do now - no plan whatsoever, to be honest - but improvisation had served him well enough thus far. He stood up and peered over the edge of the parapet into the courtyard below. It was deserted. Ramshackle lean-to buildings clung to the walls, and the usual clutter lay scattered around - a japanned carriage, a wagon laden with hay, farm implements and piles of baskets. The courtyard was overlooked on two sides by high walls and on the third by the windows of the castle buildings. On the fourth side, a low wall built along the very edge of the crag provided a spectacular view over Karnstein forest.

Talbot scanned the battlements. The only way down seemed to be through a wooden door in the wall of the west tower. He ran along to the end of the walkway and tried it. It was locked.

"Damn!" he muttered.

There was no way down but to scale the wall again. At least the descent was a little easier this side, with more and larger hand and foot holds to be found in the rough stonework. With a sigh of resignation he lowered himself over the parapet and began to climb down.

The going was slow, for he was tired after his ascent, and many of the protruding flints he was using to aid his descent were loose in the ancient mortar. Half-way down he heard the creak of a door opening in the courtyard below. He froze and peered over his shoulder.

It was Renwick, taking a last look around before he made his way back down the Crag. During the long daylight hours when his Master was vulnerable to attack, he liked to make sure that the castle was secure before he left for the village.

Renwick was tired, but happy. The Master had been pleased with the visitors the curate had brought him; so pleased that he had saved the best one to join his brides this coming evening. By way of reward he had allowed the curate to play a few sadistic games with the others before he had finished them off. He had even given Renwick a nip on the neck.

On the rare occasions when the Count granted the curate this ultimate pleasure, he was always careful not to get carried away. Renwick was no use to him dead. Or undead. Alive, he was able to mix unsuspected amongst the villagers, and do his Master's bidding under the withering light of the noonday sun.

So far Renwick had not noticed Talbot spread-eagled halfway up the far wall. Talbot tightened his grip. He felt the flint under his right foot move as the mortar cracked around it. He shifted his weight to the other foot.

Renwick walked across the courtyard and stopped directly under Talbot. Talbot watched helplessly as specks of mortar drifted down towards the curate. Cold sweat ran down his face and threatened to drip from his nose. Oblivious, Renwick gathered an armful of hay from the cart and carried it into the stables. A minute later he emerged again and headed back towards the door. He was through and closing it behind him when Talbot's foothold finally gave way. The stone fell silently then shattered on the cobbles with a crack and a clatter that echoed around the courtyard. Talbot didn't need to look to know that the game was up and started clambering back up the wall as fast as he could.

In his panic, every stone he reached out for seemed to come away in his hand. They fell all around him, filling the courtyard with sharp reports as they hit the ground. Talbot lost his footing and dangled in mid-air, legs thrashing like an epileptic puppet.

Renwick ran back into the Great Hall, his cloak raising clouds of dust, and picked a medieval crossbow from the wall. Grabbing a handful of steel-tipped bolts from the nimbus of arrows that ran around the edge of the display, he ran back outside.

Meanwhile, Talbot had recovered his hold and had nearly climbed up to the top of the wall. He leapt, twisting in mid-air, and caught hold of the lip of the parapet.

He had swung a leg over the overhang and was clambering up to safety when an agonizing shock froze his right arm. He glanced at his shoulder. A shiny arrowhead jutted out through his bicep. His leg slipped from the greasy stone and he hung for a moment by the fingertips of his left hand; then he lost his grip and fell.

* * *

Talbot's body landed with a thump in the hay cart. Renwick reloaded the crossbow and cautiously approached the wagon. He was confident that there wouldn't be much fight left in the trespasser, but he hoped that he wasn't quite dead yet. It would be nice to have a little fun with him.

The stranger had disappeared into the hay. Renwick prodded at it with the crossbow, but felt nothing. He dropped the weapon to his side and started digging through the hay, tossing it aside by the armful.

A hairy hand shot out and grabbed him by the wrist. The curate cried out in surprise, and tried to pull away. A face burst into view and he screamed again.

Until this moment, Renwick had believed that he had plumbed the most abysmal depths of fear in the service of his Master, but in the last seconds of his life he was granted the privilege of experiencing an even greater terror still. The face was that of a monstrous hybrid, part human, part wolf. Hair sprouted visibly as he watched, growing in waves across its skin. Its facial muscles writhed and swelled and, as Renwick gawped, distorted its mouth into an impossible snarl. The monster pulled the curate so close that Renwick could hear the grinding of its teeth as they grew in its jaws.

"You... shouldn't have... done that!" Talbot managed to gasp, before the red tide overwhelmed him.

Renwick struggled to free himself from the werewolf's vice-like grip. Ignoring his efforts as though they were the strugglings of a naughty child, the creature grasped the bloody arrowhead in his arm and with a sudden wrench pulled the bolt right through its shoulder and out. Blood spurted from the wound and spattered the Renwick's face. The creature let out a roar of pain and tightened its hold on the curate's forearm. The bones snapped like twigs and Renwick screamed; a reedy squeal, like the cry of a rodent.

The crossbow slipped from his grasp and clattered to the cobbles beside him.

* * *

When Talbot came to his senses again it was late in the day, and the sun was low in the sky. He tried to sit up, and winced. His right arm was aching and stiff. Blood seeped sluggishly from the wound in his shoulder. He flexed his elbow experimentally and let out an involuntary cry.

But Talbot's physical pain was as nothing in comparison to his inner anguish. He had never suffered two transformations in a single day before. He could only hope that this second attack had been triggered by the pain and shock of the wound, for the only other possibility was that his condition was worsening. Whatever the cause, the quick succession of attacks had left him dazed and confused, uncertain as to what had happened last night and what today; what was nightmare and what living nightmare.

The wound was a useful grounding in memory, however. The last thing he could remember was his giddy, panicky climb back up the wall: then the shock of pain, and the glint of the sunlight upon the steel barb protruding through his shoulder.

Once again he was smeared with blood. His own, certainly, but far more than his wound alone could account for. He looked around for some clue as to what creature it might have sprung from, and gasped in horror.

The entire courtyard was awash with gore. The hay was sodden with it. Blood spattered the walls and gathered in puddles on the cobbles. It was as though a red wave had broken over the castle and flooded the courtyard in a gory tide. Bloody bones and gobbets of unrecognisable flesh lay scattered about the scarlet pools like jetsam, and in the middle of courtyard, the remains of a body, such as it was; no more than a bloody ruin of ribs and vertebrae lying in a heap of offal.

Word had got round amongst the ravens that there was a free meal at the castle today, after all. Already, dozens were picking their way delicately through the carnage like beachcombers, their sharp eyes searching for the next morsel even before they had gulped down the last. The courtyard hummed with the ecstatic chorus of thousands of flies as they glutted themselves in an orgy of greed.

Something fixed to the side of the hay wagon caught Talbot's eye. He rose unsteadily to his feet and made his way, stumbling, through the bloodbath towards it. It was a human head; the head of the man who had shot him. The same crossbow bolt that had pierced his arm had been thrust through one eye, pinning it to the side of the cart. Talbot wiped his eyes, leaving a bloody smear across his face.

The crossbow was lying on the cobbles beside the hay cart. He picked it up, hefting it in his left hand. It was still loaded. It made him feel a little less vulnerable, trespassing in this evil place. Frightened, exhausted but purposeful, he stalked across the courtyard and through the door, into the castle buildings.

Chapter 9

In the kitchen of the Abbey House Joachim sat by the fire, drying his breeches. Dominique took the kettle off the hob and topped up the coffee pot, then filled a silver jug with hot water for the Doctor's gin. When she returned from the library, Joachim raised his eyebrows inquisitively.

"He's still in a foul mood," she replied, putting the tray down on the sideboard. "What upset him so much?"

In an elegant mime, Joachim re-enacted their fruitless search for the mummy. Dominique nodded throughout, clarifying his account with the occasional question. She had an almost telepathic bond with Joachim, and when the two of them were alone together he virtually forgot that he was mute. But then the Princess had so many curious talents.

Joachim had first laid eyes on her as he stood in line, waiting to be sold in a Haitian slave market. She had been standing a few places ahead of him, eyes cast down. She was tiny, no bigger than an adolescent, with skin of deep and glossy brown and thick, unruly hair tied back in a complex braid. Beneath her long lashes, eyes the shape and colour of almonds glittered with dark fire. She clutched a few rags of clothing to her body, protecting herself from the stares of the slavers.

She must have felt Joachim's presence, for she turned suddenly and looked up at him. A smile flickered across her face, before being snuffed out as rough hands grasped her by the shoulder and dragged her up onto the wooden stage.

The dealers had not been able to conceal the hunger in their eyes as they had stumbled over each other to open the bidding. Her price had spiralled fast and by the time the hammer fell she had fetched a small fortune.

Her new owner, a short, pot-bellied Portuguese plantation owner, seemed happy enough with the transaction. As his man returned from the stage leading Dominique by the wrist, he leered at her, exposing rotten teeth. When she stood before him, staring down at the dust, he cupped his hand under her chin and forced her head up, so that her eyes met his own. Joachim clenched his powerful fists and strained against his chains. A guard gave him a warning flick on the shoulder with his whip.

The Portuguese had given the order for his party to make ready for their departure. As his men chained his new slaves together, he kept Dominique by his side. She would share his mount.

Joachim watched disconsolately as the party prepared to leave, and hardly noticed when the guards slipped his shackles off the chain and led him up onto the stage. The auctioneer's patter droned unheeded in his ear like the buzz of an insect. Only when the bidding recommenced, did Joachim's attention returned to his own plight.

In the wake of the previous sale, the bidding started sluggishly. Joachim was tall, though, and broad at the shoulder, with an intelligence that shone through in his face. He would make a fine acquisition as a worker, a sire or even as a plaything. Before long the bidding rose to a respectable level and the idle speculators in search of a bargain dropped off one by one. Eventually only two bidders remained: the owner of the biggest cane plantation in Haiti, a hard man, used to getting his own way; and a stout widow who made no secret of her reasons for staying in the bidding. She played to the crowd, licking her lips, rolling her eyes and calling for the auctioneer to lift Joachim's loincloth.

Even without any understanding of the Portuguese in which these ribaldries had been exchanged, Joachim was aware that his fate hung in the balance between a life of back breaking labour or one of grotesque sexual servitude. Finally, the sheer spending power of the cane farmer frustrated the widow. With a torrent of ear curling abuse at her rival she gathered up her skirts and stumped angrily out of the square, the jeers of the crowd ringing in her ear.

The auctioneer looked around the crowd for final bids. Joachim found himself doing the same, hoping desperately that some benefactor might offer him a future less bleak. Nobody cared to take on the cane farmer.

As the auctioneer raised his gavel, a voice from the back of the crowd raised the bid. Everybody looked round. It was the plantation owner, with Dominique beside him. His face was blank and expressionless, his voice strangely distant. Irritated by this new intervention, the farmer raised his bid. Dominique leant close to her new owner and whispered in his ear. In the same monotonous voice the Portuguese topped the bid again.

As the bidding rose a buzz went around the crowd. The farmer grew purple as every bid he made was immediately bettered by the plantation owner. All the while, the Portuguese continued to stare blankly ahead, only opening his mouth to bid. Dominique stood by his side, an almost imperceptible smile playing across her lips.

In the end, the farmer's business sense overcame his ego and he turned away from the stage, feigning unconcern as the auctioneer rapped his gavel and pointed to the Portuguese.

The action seemed to wake the plantation owner from his trance, for he rubbed his eyes and looked around, confused and bewildered. It took him a moment to comprehend that he had just spent a small fortune on a slave for whom he had no need. Unwilling to admit to a mistake in front of his staff, he hastily improvised a plausible excuse for the aberration. His man picked his way through the crowd, handed over a heavy purse with a shrug and returned with an equally bemused Joachim. Dominique sneaked him a conspiratorial smile.

The Portuguese set Dominique on as a chambermaid, while Joachim was put to work in the plantation. His tireless strength and keen intelligence immediately impressed the foreman, and it was not long before he was given supervisory responsibility over the rest of the slaves. With that came the run of the place, and the freedom to meet Dominique whenever she could escape her duties. Over the weeks their meetings become more frequent and more intimate, and the two of them had fallen in love.

Meanwhile, the plantation owner had made it clear that he expected more of Dominique than the making of the beds. For a while she managed to fob him off with a combination of calculated flirtation and the use of those strange mesmeric powers she had demonstrated at the slave market, but eventually her stratagems and ruses wore what little patience he had to breaking point.

One afternoon Joachim was in the fields, cutting cane under the gaze of an unblinking sun. The slaves were singing, swinging their machetes in time to a mournful lament, when above their dirge he heard Dominique's terrified cries. He ran from the field, still clutching his machete, and into the house, kicking his way through the doors until he reached the master bedroom.

As the last door crashed off its hinges he saw the plantation owner holding Dominique down upon the bed and tearing at her clothes. The Portuguese spun around at the commotion, then launched himself off the bed towards the dresser, upon which lay his horsewhip. He had not got half way across the room before Joachim caught him by the throat and hurled him into a corner. He collapsed to the floor, pleading for mercy, while Joachim towered over him, challenging him to stand and fight. A moment later a dozen plantation workers burst into the room and set upon Joachim, finally bringing him to the ground by sheer weight of numbers.

At the end of the working day, the rest of the slaves were assembled outside the plantation owner's house. After a long wait Dominique emerged, half-naked, bruised and beaten, and was forced to stand with the others. Then Joachim was dragged out half-conscious, his back bleeding from scores of whip lashes. The men threw him to the ground and held him down while another two of their number forced his jaws open, and a third delved inside his mouth with a pair of pincers. Then the plantation owner stepped forward. He drew his knife, bent over the struggling Joachim and with one swift stroke, silenced him forever.

* * *

The plantation workers left Joachim writhing on the ground, unconcerned whether he lived or died. It took every scrap of Dominique's remaining strength to persuade the terrified slaves to help her drag him to the sleeping quarters. Through the night she attended him, staunching the terrible wound, and helping him breathe when the swelling stump of his tongue threatened to block the passage of air. By morning the worst was over, and she collapsed beside him; both had slept through until late afternoon.

She stayed by Joachim's side for the next few days, nursing him back to health while she, too, recovered from her own beating. The plantation owner had lost interest in her for the time being, and she was allowed to come and go more or less as she pleased. Joachim, on the other hand, was returned to work as soon as he was fit enough to stand. He joined the gang obediently, head hung down. Each time he collapsed from exhaustion the overseers kicked and swore at him until he struggled back to his feet. To all appearances he was a spent force.

Meanwhile, Dominique took to wandering daily around the edges of the fields and through the banana plantations, gathering a plant here, digging up a root there. She spoke to no-one, not even the other slaves. Rumours sprung up amongst them that she was a Ju-ju Princess, and they began to avoid her glance and to keep a safe distance between from her whenever possible. Only at night would she speak, whispering secrets and incantations into the ear of Joachim as he lay beside her, staring blankly at the ceiling.

One breathless night, following a day so close that it seemed to have wrung all sustenance out of the air they breathed, the slaves were woken by the sound of Dominique's voice. Gathering clouds had covered the moon, and they could only just make out her naked body in the gloom, as she squat over the recumbent figure of Joachim, chanting softly. As she sang, she dipped her fingers into a pot of dark paste, and described strange figures and patterns upon his face and chest. The slaves huddled together at the far end of the dormitory, trembling in fear and awe.

Her chanting grew louder, until her voice had filled the hut. As her song reached its crescendo a terrible crash of thunder shook the building to its foundations, and in the brief illumination of the lightning flash, the slaves had seen her standing over Joachim, screaming her incantations into the night sky. Just as suddenly the light was gone and so was Joachim, leaving the door open wide.

Dominique walked across the room and out onto the veranda, oblivious to the panic of the slaves, who stumbled over each other in their efforts to avoid being touched by her shadow. She sat down cross-legged on the dusty boards, staring unblinking through the storm at the other buildings; the slave keepers' quarters and the plantation owner's house. The rain began to fall.

Every now and then a jagged knife of lightning slashed through the night sky, followed by an earth-shaking crash of thunder. The other slaves gathered in the doorway behind Dominique.

Then a light appeared, livid and flickering, in one of the windows of the plantation owner's house, growing brighter until a tongue of flame had leapt up from one of the roofs. The slaves broke into a flurry of excited chatter, but all stayed rooted in the doorway, watching as the conflagration grew to engulf the building and moved swiftly on to the others. Distant cries and the rattle of gunfire drifted across the compound, dying away eventually to leave no sound but the crackle of the flames and the steady hiss of the rain. As they watched, the roof of plantation owner's house collapsed, sending a cloud of golden sparks into the night sky.

The slaves looked at each other, their faces blank with shock and bewilderment. No-one knew what to do, nor even whether there was anything to do. Dominique, the only person who seemed to have any sense of purpose, continued to sit on the verandah, staring out into the night.

Then a figure appeared, silhouetted against the blazing buildings. It strode towards the slave's quarters, causing panic among them as it approached. It was only a few yards away when a final flash of lightning, the last defiant blast of the spent storm, illuminated it for a moment. It was Joachim.

His eyes were glazed and unfocussed and his face and body slick with blood. The rain beat down upon his half-naked body, running down his legs and leaving a crimson trail in his wake. His hands hung limp by his side, one holding a dripping machete, the other still clutching blood-sodden shreds of what might have been clothing, but which were probably not. He stood before Dominique for a moment, swaying slightly, then, like some mighty ebony tree before the woodsman's axe, crashed face first into the mud.

* * *

Dominique let him sleep for a couple of hours, lying beside him, silently watching, as she had done before. As soon as he woke, Dominique urged him to collect together anything that might help them on their way. While he sorted out food and blankets, she walked over to the ruins of the plantation owner's house and dug around in the steaming ashes, returning laden with items she had recovered from the fire; a musket, flask and shot, some silver, even one or two pieces of clothing which had escaped the flames. They packed everything they had collected into two saddle bags and rode out just before dawn, on the Portuguese's stallion.

Only when they had left the ruins of the plantation far behind them did Dominique reach around Joachim's broad barrel of a chest and wave a small, heavy leather purse under his nose.

"Gold!" she laughed above the rush of the wind and the clatter of the horse's hooves, "back pay!"

It was enough to buy them an illicit passage on the first boat out of Porto Prince, which was by chance a clipper to Copenhagen. From there they hired a fishing boat to ferry them across the Baltic to mainland Europe, and made their way overland to Berlin, heading for the Mediterranean and eventually Africa.

By whatever mysterious agency bad news spreads, the story of the plantation massacre had preceded them, and handbills offering a bounty for their arrest were posted at all the ports and staging posts. Twice they narrowly escaped capture, the second time only by jumping from the balcony of a dilapidated lodging house and fleeing through the backstreets, leaving behind the few possessions they owned.

They arrived in Prague as winter drew in. Tired and destitute, and unable to seek work, they were forced to sleep on the streets and to scavenge what food they could. Dominique had fallen prey to the cold, and Joachim had no money to buy the medicines and warm clothes she needed to recover her strength. Untreated, her condition worsened, until she had fallen into a fever, crying out in her delirium of the horrors of the plantation.

One frosty morning as Joachim lay shivering on a park bench under a single threadbare blanket, pressing his body against Dominique's to keep her warm, a party of the civil militia had swooped upon them. They demanded to see the couple's travelling documents and indentures. Taking Joachim's silence for insolence, they were reaching for their billy clubs when a shrill voice cut through the stillness of the morning.

"Where the bloody hell have you been?"

All turned to see a diminutive figure striding across the street, angrily waving his stick in the air. Ignoring the militia men, Doctor Pretorius (for it was he) poked Joachim in the chest and said, "I've been walking the streets all bloody night looking for you."

He prodded the recumbent form of Dominique with his stick.

"Get up, damn you woman!" he ordered. Even in her delirium, Dominique vaguely understood that the stranger was acting in their best interests and managed somehow to stagger to her feet. Pretorius leant towards her, peering suspiciously over the rims of his spectacles.

"Have you been drinking again?" he snapped, "because if you have, so help me I'll - I'll - "

Dominique stared at Pretorius in blank bewilderment then turned and huddled into Joachim's warm side. The Doctor addressed the officer in charge of the militia men, acknowledging their presence for the first time.

"Bloody servants!" he exclaimed, withering the sergeant under the blast of his halitosis. "Who'd have 'em, eh? Eh?"

The sergeant stepped back a pace.

"Am I to understand that these two cannibals are your servants, Herr... - "

" - Count Saint-Germain, Bavarian Charge d'Affaires" Pretorius had lied grandly, "travelling without retinue on an affair of state."

He leant towards the sergeant and lowered his voice.

"A matter of some delicacy," he added, winking conspiratorially.

He straightened back up.

"As this is the first time my pet savages have visited your magnificent Capitol, I made the mistake of giving them the evening off to see the sights. And this - " he jabbed Joachim again - "is the thanks I get."

The sergeant moved back another pace. Around him his men had started to smirk at the self-important little bureaucrat who could not even keep discipline among his own staff. The sergeant paused for a moment, in some confusion as to what to do.

"Very well, Herr Count, I will take no further action against these two. I trust, however, that you will make it clear to them that ours is a civilised city, and that we do not expect visitors to go around without papers or to sleep on the streets. Good morning."

And with that he saluted, just to be on the safe side, and marched his men off down the street. Pretorius winked at Joachim.

"Gullible tossers," he said under his breath.

Pretorius had in fact merely been walking off a hangover, and had saved the two fugitives on a momentary whim.

He beckoned to Joachim and set off down the street. Joachim gathered Dominique into his arms and followed the Doctor back to the apartments he rented above his laboratory on the Glubenstrasse.

Pretorius fed them, gave them a room, and mixed Dominique the medicines she needed. When, eventually she recovered and, trusting Pretorius for want of any alternative, had confessed their dilemma to him, he had made them a proposal: they could stay with him as long as they wished, working as his cook and manservant. He would provide them with bed and board and pay them what he could. There would be no contracts, and they would be free to leave whenever they wished.

It was an arrangement which suited both parties. Joachim and Dominique had somewhere to live, and the means by which to save for the last leg of their journey. Pretorius was able at last to engage and retain the services of a brace of servants. His researches into the hermetic arts involved the generation of a variety of foul smells and regular loud explosions, and servants tended to be a superstitious lot. The three settled down into a comfortable working relationship, and before long become quite attached to each other.

In the small hours of one January morning a particularly loud explosion blew the front off the laboratory and shattered windows up and down the street. Joachim was thrown bodily out of bed. He and Dominique rushed downstairs, expecting the worst. They had found Pretorius sitting in the ruins of his laboratory, his face black with soot but otherwise unhurt. Joachim picked the Doctor out of the debris while Dominique found the old man's spectacles and replaced them on his nose. Meanwhile, the owners of what was left of the neighbouring houses emerged into the street in their night clothes. The initial wave of sympathy towards the Doctor, based on the general impression that there had been a bomb attack upon him, soon gave way to open hostility as they realised that the explosion had been of his own making. Things might have turned nasty had Joachim not started to ostentatiously lift the heaviest beams out of the rubble and hurl them aside. The crowd dispersed slowly, with some residents muttering darkly about legal action.

Pretorius thought it better to leave Prague without delay. Aspects of his activities were not entirely legal, and he did not wish to find himself in the position of having to explain himself to the authorities. He set out to find some forgotten backwater where he could continue his studies undisturbed, and settled on Karnstein. Joachim and Dominique, who had not yet saved enough to complete their journey, went with him.

In Karnstein there was even less for them to spend their money on than there had been in Prague, and it had not taken them long to save all they needed to complete their journey home. Now they continued to serve the Doctor only until they had repaid the outstanding debt of gratitude they owed him for his generosity and fair dealing.

Little could they know just how soon the opportunity to do so would arise, nor could they conceive the scale of the tragedy that would follow in its wake.

Chapter 10

Michael sat despondently on the bank of the Farkle, wringing out his hose. After finding the sarcophagus empty, Pretorius had been unapproachable; and rather than risk the possibility of being thrown to Joachim, Michael had decided to defer asking for his reward. He had waited at a discreet distance while they had loaded the crate into the trap and set off back to the Abbey House. Now he was alone, no better off than he had been a couple of hours ago and short of a boot. He sighed.

He tucked the damp bundle into his remaining boot, tied it to his belt by the laces, and set off barefoot along the river bank. Perhaps, he speculated, Tom might stand him a pint. In all conscience though, or at least in what little conscience God had seen fit to bestow upon him, he could think of no reason why he should.

He had not walked far when he stopped short. Twenty yards ahead of him, a child was playing by the river's edge. Michael dropped into a rheumatic crouch.

Many years ago he had discovered that children were a valuable resource. Their pockets were always bulging, often with rubbish, but also with apples, wedges of cheese or ends of sausage. Sometimes they even had the odd groat as well. Through the application of guile, or when that failed, imaginative threats, he was sometimes able to part them from their possessions.

He scrambled up the bank and crept along under cover of the shrubbery until he was right behind the little girl. Even from behind there was no mistaking the ginger curls of Maude Bumblewicz, rosy-cheeked apple of the Bumblewiczes' eyes. She was kneeling at the edge of the bank, wholly absorbed in her game, picking flowers and floating the heads down the river one by one.

Michael rubbed his hands together in unholy glee. Here was an ideal opportunity to square relations with one and all, including the Bumblewiczes, whilst at the same time indulging in a little harmless fun. All he had to do was to sneak up on the brat unseen and shove her into the river, retire behind the bushes while she squawked and swallowed a little water, then appear on the bank at the last minute to rescue her. That he could not swim was no impediment: he had no intention of getting wet anyway. The bank was littered with branches that he could use to drag her out.

He crept out of the bushes, and was almost upon her when a twig snapped under his knee with a resounding crack. Maude turned to find Michael's face mere inches from her own. With a strangled shriek of surprise she recoiled, lost her footing and plunged into the river.

Michael had not intended to reveal himself so early in the proceedings, but circumstances forced his hand. He selected a suitable branch and reached out towards her.

"Grab hold of this, Maudy girl. I'll save you," he said, waggling the end enticingly.

"Go away," replied Maude, treading water. "Daddy thayth that you're a dithguthting old man and that I muthn't talk to you."

She turned around in the water and swam confidently towards the far bank.

Michael was buggered if he was going to see his chance of becoming a hero snatched from under his nose by the very whelp he was trying to rescue. Without further thought he threw down the branch and leapt in after her.

Maude reached the bank and clambered out of the water. Behind her, Michael struggled as far as the middle of the river before panic set in. He flailed his arms wildly and tried to shout for help, but the moment he opened his mouth, half the river seemed to rush in.

Maude watched with interest as the old man floundered, debating whether or not to help him. She was a logical child. As things stood, if her clothes were not dry by evening she would be in trouble enough with her mother. If she rescued Michael, she would then have to explain what she was doing by the river when she had been expressly forbidden from playing there. Anyway, she reasoned, it was his own silly fault for going round creeping up on people.

She sat down on the bank and spread her skirts to catch the warmth of the noonday sun. She continued to watch Michael thrash helplessly in the water until the current swept him round the next bend and out of sight.

* * *

Father Shandor was troubled. Having discharged his ecclesiastical and pastoral duties for the morning he had set off for a walk along the riverbank. He needed time to come to terms with the horror he had witnessed last night, and he wanted to pursue his meditations far from the temptation of the bottle. Many years ago, when he had first encountered the Count, he had suffered a terrible crisis of faith. Then, he had turned to drink. It had nearly killed him. This time he was determined not to fall into the same trap.

But there was more to think about besides; other clues he must try to piece together if he was to understand the undertow of events.

A strange noise dragged him from the solitude of his thoughts. He stopped, and cocked an ear. There it was again; a rushing sound, reminiscent of water going down a drain. He looked around and was surprised to see Michael float past, waving. He waved back.

The sight of the old man anywhere near water was unusual enough for the Father to take a second look. At a second glance, he realised that Michael was getting lower in the water with each passing moment.

He picked up a branch and ran after the old man, overtook him and lowered it into his path. Michael made a desperate grab for it and held on tight. Shandor hauled him towards the bank, then abandoned the branch and dragged the old man out of the water by his belt.

"You seem to be making something of a habit of this, Michael," he said.

Unable for the moment to reply, Michael nodded weakly and threw up.

Chapter 11

Talbot's eyes took a moment to adjust to the gloom.

The dust on the floor of the Great Hall had been recently disturbed by several sets of footprints, more than could be accounted for by the attacker who lay distributed around the courtyard. Among the tracks he could make out the marks of women's shoes. Perhaps Connie's party had passed this way. The table bore the evidence of a recent meal. Six places were set, though only five had been used.

Talbot tucked a dagger from one of the weapon displays into his belt, and armed himself with some more crossbow bolts from another.

At one end of the hall, sweeping staircases branched left and right to a gallery that ran around the walls. Talbot took the left-hand flight and started to explore the next floor.

Leading off from the gallery was a long corridor with doors to either side. Most were locked, but a few opened into furnished bedrooms showing signs of recent occupation. In the first room the bedclothes were thrown about, as if someone had tossed and turned through an uncomfortable night; in another the bowl had been filled and a towel lay discarded upon a nearby chair. Talbot's hopes began to rise that he might find his friends unharmed after all.

In the next chamber those hopes were dashed. The room was in disarray, as if it had witnessed a desperate struggle. The furniture had been overturned and, in one corner, a lamp lay shattered in a pool of oil. More worrying still was the crimson stain spread across the white coverlet of the bed.

Talbot rushed out of the room and down the corridor, kicking open doors to left and right, and calling his fiancé's name. At the end of the corridor a rough wooden door opened onto a spiral staircase that wound up into impenetrable gloom.

He started up the stone stairs, his back pressed to the damp wall, alert to the possibility of attack from above. Before long he had left what little light there had been far behind him, and continued his dizzying ascent in pitch darkness.

He was on the verge of abandoning the climb when his head bumped against a wooden obstruction. He explored the mildewed surface with his fingers and found the outline of a trapdoor. Bracing his left shoulder against it, he heaved it up and over. It fell back onto the floor of the room above with a crash, sending dust billowing down through the opening. He raised his head and shoulders through the trap.

Cool evening air caressed his face. It was dusk, and he found himself looking out between the columns of a stone balustrade at the dull orange glow left in the western skies by the setting sun. Eight stone arches commanded a panoramic view of the surrounding countryside. He had climbed up into the watchtower.

As he stood looking down into the valley below, a drop of moisture splashed his cheek. As he casually brushed it away, he caught sight of his fingertips. They were smeared with red. He looked up.

Above his head hung a great bronze bell and bound to the clapper, the body of a young woman. Her arms swung gently in the evening breeze, her fingertips almost brushing his hair. Her face was encrusted with dried blood, which had flowed from a gaping knife wound across her throat. Rusty rivulets ran down her arms; a last few drops still hung from her fingers. Talbot gasped in horror; but a moment later cried out aloud in pain and grief when he recognised the blood-sodden countenance as that of Victoria, Constance's travelling companion.

* * *

Talbot was still reeling from his discovery when a hand closed around his ankle and dragged him down through the trap. Perhaps his unseen assailant had been expecting more resistance; for as Talbot fell back, he too lost his balance, and the pair tumbled end over end down the stairs. Around and around they went, crashing into the walls and each other, gathering speed like rag dolls thrown down a helter skelter. At the bottom of the steps they burst through the narrow doorway and came to a halt in a tangle of limbs.

Though dizzy and dazed, Talbot managed to stagger to his feet before his attacker recovered. He had lost his crossbow in the fall. He reached for his dagger. That, too, had gone. The crossbow bolts lay broken and splintered on the floor.

Talbot's assailant rolled over, and sat up. As he did so, twilight from a narrow window fell upon his face.

"Ajax!" Talbot exclaimed, for even in the half-light he recognised the stout figure and mild countenance of Constance's younger brother, Ajax Quigley, "you are alive!"

"Only just," Ajax groaned. He peered at Talbot myopically, for he had lost his spectacles in his fall.

Talbot helped his friend to his feet. Ajax made to embrace him, but even as he did, some prudent instinct made Talbot step back.

Ajax' face had twisted into a mask of bestial hunger, and his lips curled back into a snarl. Elongated, razor-sharp incisors gleamed in the dark. With a serpent-like hiss he threw himself upon Talbot.

The two collapsed to the ground, Ajax' fingers entangled in Talbot's hair, wrenching his head back to expose his neck. The veins swelled upon Talbot's trembling arm as he clutched at Ajax' throat, straining to hold back those savage jaws. But exhaustion, shock and loss of blood had all taken their toll on him. Slowly but inexorably, Ajax' superhuman strength was overwhelming his own. Ajax' gaping maw was now so close to Talbot's face that he could feel the vampire's cold breath upon his cheek, and smell the taint of death.

Talbot's right hand clawed frantically at the floor, searching for something with which to defend himself. His numb fingers closed around one of the crossbow bolts. Although the steel arrowhead had snapped off, the break had left a jagged splinter. With his last ounce of strength Talbot plunged the shaft into Ajax' back.

Ajax arched his back, shrieking in pain and rage, then rolled off Talbot to lie face up on the floor.

Ajax was still breathing, but from his irregular, sobbing gasps Talbot knew that his undeath was fading fast. The demonic glint had gone from his eyes and the familiar, albeit faint, life-spark of Connie's brother had returned.

"Oh, Ajax!" Talbot sobbed, clutching his friend's hand.   "What have I done?"

"You...have saved my...soul," Ajax managed to whisper. Then his eyes opened wide, filled with horror. His fingernails dug into Talbot's palm.

"Connie!" he exclaimed hoarsely. "She still lives! HE is saving her...to take for his bride...tonight. You must rescue her!"

Ajax words were lost in a paroxysm of racking coughs. A dribble of blood trickled from the corner of his mouth.

"Easy, dear friend," Talbot murmured soothingly. "Do not exert yourself. You must rest until I can fetch help."

"Too...late for that...thank God. You must go to...Constance...in the catacombs. Be careful...he is down there...for your sake I pray... that he is still sleeping. Go! Go now! And God go with you..."

Again the pain overwhelmed him. More blood bubbled from his mouth; then his body relaxed and he slumped back, to breathe no more.

* * *

Talbot clasped the body of his young friend to his chest, rocking him gently as if he were lulling a baby to sleep. A solitary tear trickled down his cheek.

Ajax' words still rang in his ears. His dear Connie was in danger, held in the catacombs of the castle by - by what? He did not know, dared not imagine. Nevertheless, whatever the danger, he would find her, or die in the attempt. Gently he laid Ajax' body down on the floor and clambered to his feet.

He had to find the catacombs. He continued to run along the seemingly endless succession of corridors, innumerable cobwebby rooms, and countless dead ends with ever greater urgency. The gathering evening plunged the castle still deeper into darkness.

In one room he could just make out signs of habitation through the gloom. After a brief, fumbling search he found a tinderbox and lit a candle. On the table beside the candle the black contents of a lidded jar suddenly swirled into activity. Talbot lifted the jar and looked closer. It was full of flies. Talbot shuddered, and left the room. The candle cast eerie shadows along the corridors, but Talbot was grateful nonetheless for its flickering light.

At last he descended a twisting staircase, the stone steps worn into soft curves by centuries of use, into a gloomy hall and was confronted by a pair of mighty, mouldering doors, guarded on either side by mounted suits of armour. A cool draught squeezed through the cracks and touched his face, prickling the hair on the nape of his neck.

Talbot lifted the heavy iron rings and pulled. The doors swung inwards with a mournful groan, and a blast of cold air rushed out to greet him, laden with the musty odour of decay. His skin crawled. He had found the entrance to the catacombs at last.

The candle flame reared away as if in fear. Talbot cupped the guttering spark in his hand, protecting it from the draught. Beyond the doors, another flight of crumbling stone steps disappeared into the gloom. He slowed his pace, partly because the steps were uneven, partly in apprehension of what he might find below.

At the bottom of the stairs the catacombs stretched out before him into the darkness. Thick stone pillars supported a ceiling so lofty that the candlelight barely reached the vaulting. He shouted Connie's name. Echoes swooped around his head like bats and died away to silence, broken only by the drip of water from the roof. He crept forward between rows of pillars, glancing over his shoulder frequently to make sure that his escape route was still in view.

Then, ahead of him, he saw a vague shape through the darkness; and as he got nearer, recognised the brown of Constance's travelling cape. She lay, unmoving, on the flat slab atop an ancient tomb. For a moment Talbot thought she was dead. He touched her cheek, and felt a reassuring warmth. Closer, he could also see the gentle rise and fall of her breast. Talbot murmured her name and, when that failed to arouse her, shook by the shoulder; but to no avail. Whatever spell had been cast over her had taken her beyond his reach.

The sides of the tomb upon which she lay bore emblems similar to those Talbot had seen above the drawbridge and throughout the castle, the coat of

116

arms of the Drakul clan. Grotesque bat-winged gargoyles kept watch from each corner of the tomb.

What was that? Talbot thought that he heard a sound. He raised the candle high and peered into the fathomless dark all around him. He could see nothing. Yet a moment later he heard the sound again, a faint rustle, like somebody turning over in bed. He put his ear to the stone. Fear dragged icy fingers down his back. The sound was coming from within the tomb itself.

The candle dropped from his hand, rolled across the slab and fell to the floor. Instantly, the catacombs were plunged into utter darkness. Talbot gathered his fiancé into his arms. As he picked her up, her weight bore down on his wounded shoulder and he cursed at the pain. Shifting the greater part of her weight to his good arm, he staggered blindly into the void, heading in what he hoped was the direction of the staircase.

More than once he crashed into the stone pillars, bruising himself and his precious cargo indiscriminately. But the pillars proved his salvation. By progressing from one to the next he held to a straight course, until at last he stumbled upon the bottom step of the staircase.

He staggered up the stairs and slammed the heavy doors behind him. Laying Constance gently down upon the floor, he removed a broadsword from the grasp of one of the sentinel suits of armour, and thrust it through the rings of the door. That, he thought, should delay any pursuit by whatever lurked in the tomb below.

Gathering Constance back into his arms he made his through the maze of the castle buildings and out across the moonlit courtyard to the gatehouse. The drawbridge chains were wound around two broad wooden drums, held in check by a brake lever. Talbot pulled the lever. The drum started, slowly, to turn, unspooling its load of clanking chains. Outside, the drawbridge descended with gathering speed, and hit the ground on the far side of the moat with a crash loud enough to wake the dead. Talbot staggered out of the gatehouse and across the drawbridge. He did not look back.

Chapter 12

Evening had fallen, and the Crow & Gibbet was filling up. Michael sat alone in the corner with a tankard in his hand and a face glazed with sad stupefaction, drinking his way through the money he had wheedled out of Shandor for a new pair of boots.

Nobody was talking to him. Most of the villagers had heard one version or another of the corpse-robbing incident; others were wary – wrongly, for once - of the puddle that was collecting under his bench. He was still extremely moist, particularly in those nooks and crannies where the afternoon sun had not been able to penetrate.

He was thinking about life or, to be more precise, that series of humiliations laid end to end which passed for his own life. What, he was in the process of asking himself, had he done with it so far? Nothing, he was obliged to reply. Talbot was half his age and a loony to boot: that had not preventing the young master from travelling the world. He had been to places and seen things that Michael could never dream of. Neither was Michael ever going to receive crates from Eejit, or organise search parties, or even run an inn.

When Tom called last orders, the patrons would all drink up and straggle back to their homes, to be belaboured by their wives or to belabour their children. What would he do? Stagger off to spend the night jostling with livestock in a barn, perhaps, or maybe just crawl under a bush.

The only event of his life in which he had ever taken any pride had been the birth of his son. Admittedly, he had been unconscious in a midden at the time of the happy event. Neither had he ever made a contribution to the lad's welfare, nor played any part in his upbringing. Nonetheless, he had known that the boy was his own, the one good thing he could point to and say that he had played a part in creating. Even that had been taken from him. A tear rolled slowly down his cheek.

Many and varied though Michael's faults were, he was not one to wallow in self-pity. He wiped his nose on the back of his sleeve, sniffed, and rose unsteadily to his feet. He was making his way towards the bar when the door burst open and Talbot staggered in, bloodstained and dishevelled, carrying the lifeless body of his fiancé, Constance, the lady with the muff.

* * *

There is nothing sobers a man up quicker than being confronted by a violent lunatic carrying what appears to be a corpse. Michael shot across the room like a cork out of a bottle, leapt over the bar and landed head-first in Tom's slop pail. After a couple of restorative swallows of the contents he disentangled himself from the handle and peered cautiously over the edge of the bar.

Talbot laid his burden down on the nearest trestle and collapsed onto the bench beside it. The villagers who had been drinking around the table fell over each other in their efforts to keep a safe distance between themselves and him. Talbot's face and chest were caked in dried blood and dirt, his hands and feet were scratched and torn, and blood oozed sluggishly from the wound in his arm. He looked every inch the madman.

He smashed his fist down on the tabletop. The entire clientele jumped as one.

"Fetch a doctor!" he ordered, his eyes blazing, "and bring me food and drink. Now!"

Tom hurried to fill a tankard. One of the villagers edged towards the door, slipped out and set off down the road. Tom approached Talbot's table cautiously, set down the tankard and a joint of mutton, and backed away. Talbot picked up the joint and started to eat ravenously.

"Is s-she dead?" someone asked. Talbot looked up from his feast.

"No," he replied, "but I cannot rouse her."

"Any wounds?" asked Tom, nervously.

"None that I can find," said Talbot taking a draught of ale.

"No marks or scars?" continued Tom.

"No."

"Show us her neck," came a voice from a dark corner.

Exasperated by this barrage of questions, Talbot pulled down Constance's collar. Those at the back of the crowd stood on tiptoe to search her neck for any sign of the vampire's bite. Satisfied at last that she was unmarked, there was a general relaxation all round.

"What about her tits, then?" asked Yeoman Muller hopefully. Talbot glared at him. Michael stood up.

"So are you still loony, then, young master?"

"Michael!" Talbot exclaimed, with something akin to pleasure, "I thought you were...well, never mind. Good to see you, anyway. My mental state is much improved, thank you, but as you can see, the same cannot be said for my body. Perhaps somebody might find me some bandages."

Tom rummaged behind the bar and produced a grubby glass cloth. He flung it across to Talbot. Talbot tried to tear the cloth into bandages, but his right hand was numb and useless.

"I'll do that," said Michael, stepping round the bar. Talbot regarded him uncertainly.

"Are you sure you know what you're doing?" he asked.

"Garn! Nothing to it!" Michael scoffed. Talbot reluctantly handed him the cloth. Michael started tearing it into strips.

* * *

Shandor heard Talbot's cry of pain from half way down the street. He redoubled his pace, leaving behind the villager who had summoned him from his bed. By the time he reached the Crow & Gibbet, Talbot had snatched the bandages back from Michael and was trying to apply them himself. Michael was rubbing the side of his head and looking aggrieved.

"T'was bound to hurt a bit," he was muttering to no-one in particular, "still no reason to clout a fellow."

Shandor checked Connie's pulse and, to Talbot's irritation, inspected her neck again. Satisfied that she was in no immediate danger, he took over the bandaging operation himself.

"You must tell me everything that has happened," he commanded as he swabbed Talbot's wound with brandy. Do not omit a single detail."

"It can wait," replied Talbot, wincing, but forebearing from settling the same treatment upon the Father that he had dished out to Michael. "My first concern is to get Connie seen by a doc."

"Your fiancé may already be beyond the reach of medical science," said Shandor, "possibly beyond any help but that of our Lord. That is why I must know everything."

"Very well. But then you must promise to help me."

"You have my word."

"Last night," Talbot began, "I suffered an attack of the mental disorder which is my curse. During that fit I must have escaped from the Burgomeister's cell - "

122

"Escape!" interjected Michael, "bloody near pulled the cell-house down on my head, begging your pardon, Father. Now, Von Trapp's after your hide and no mistaking. Trouble with you is, you don't know your own bloody strength," he added pointedly, rubbing his ear again.

Talbot ignored him and continued, describing how he had woken to find himself lying on the drawbridge of Castle Dracula, his perilous climb over the battlements and how he had come by his wound.

With dark foreboding, Shandor questioned the wounded man about the appearance of his attacker. Talbot's description left the Father in no doubt about his identity.

"Renwick," he sighed, "somehow I knew it."

The thought that a servant of the Count had been walking among them unrecognised - even acting as a servant of the church - sent a renewed *frisson* of horror through the villagers.

They pressed closer to listen as Talbot picked up his tale. He thought it judicious to gloss over the details of Renwick's bloody demise - there was no benefit to be gained from disclosing the true nature of his malady to the superstitious crowd. It was enough to suggest that during their struggle he had been forced to take his attacker's life to save his own. Shandor genuflected and whispered a prayer for his late colleague's soul.

Talbot's description of the fates of Victoria and Ajax caused a buzz of nervous chatter to break out amongst his audience. There was a general consensus that Connie's party had been given fair warning, but that on the other hand nobody, not even strangers, deserved as terrible a death as that.

Talbot fell silent, overcome by the horror of his recollections.

"Young master tells a rattling good yarn, don't he?" said Michael, admiringly.

Shandor gave him an icy stare and laid a hand upon the young man's shoulder. Talbot waved him away weakly.

"I will be all right in a minute," he said. "Perhaps I might have some spirits?"

Shandor poured the young man a measure of the brandy with which he had been swabbing his wounds and set it on the trestle before him. Talbot gulped a large mouthful and closed his eyes, enjoying the calming fire that raged briefly in his throat. The hubbub died away to silence.

"Goodness knows how I found my way down the mountainside; mortal terror is a great incentive. I half ran, half fell; ever alert to the possibility of pursuit by the monster that I had deprived of its prey. The brambles tore at Connie's clothing and at my flesh, but I scarcely noticed the wounds. At last I found myself on the outskirts of the village, and in sight of safety.

"There: I have told you everything I have to tell. Now you must keep your side of the bargain, Father."

Talbot took another sip of brandy and looked at Shandor expectantly.

Shandor made no reply. It had been many years since he had felt the devil so close. He thought he could even detect a whiff of brimstone - though it could have just been Michael - and hear the flexing of leathery wings behind the creak of the pub sign, swinging in the evening breeze.

His eyes strayed to the brandy bottle.

Chapter 13

Doctor Pretorius sat in one of the Abbey House library's leather armchairs, staring glumly into his glass. From next door came the clatter of cutlery as Joachim set the table for dinner.

Although Pretorius usually enjoyed nothing more than entertaining, it was with no great sense of pleasure that he anticipated the arrival of his guest this evening. For tonight, inevitably, the subject of their wager would arise, and Pretorius would have to admit how badly he was faring. Honesty at this stage might at least go some way towards alleviating the ignominy of his inevitable defeat.

The doorbell rang. Pretorius took a large swallow of gin and braced himself. He heard Joachim leave the dining room and tramp down the hall. A minute later the manservant knocked softly and entered the library.

Since they had taken up residence in Karnstein, Joachim had devised a system of charades for announcing callers. He held up four fingers.

"Four visitors?" repeated Pretorius, surprised.

Joachim nodded. He stroked an imaginary beard, then wagged his finger in admonishment.

"Shandor? That's a bloody nuisance."

Joachim nodded his agreement. He was aware that the Father regarded Pretorius' overdue dinner guest as one of Satan's handmaidens, and that it would be most undesirable for Shandor to discover that the Doctor was breaking bread with him.

"And the others?"

Joachim shrugged twice, then held his nose with one hand while fanning his bottom with the other.

"Two strangers and Michael," interpreted Pretorius. "You'd better see them in."

He had barely risen from his chair when the door burst open and Talbot backed into the room, with his fiancé's legs tucked under his arms. Michael followed, struggling under the weight of her upper body.

"Forgive my intrusion, sir," said Talbot, laying Constance on a convenient chaise longue, "but my arms are beginning to tire."

Ignoring Pretorius' protestations, Shandor introduced Talbot and outlined Constance's affliction. As the Father had anticipated, his description was enough to awaken the doctor's academic curiosity. A few moments later, Pretorius was bent over her, lifting her eyelids and peering at her pupils through a lens.

To the Doctor's relief, Shandor did not stay long. As soon as Pretorius had reassured him that he would take care of the patient and her fiancé, he made his apologies and left. Talbot's tale had suggested that the vampire plague was farther advanced than even he had feared. There was a great deal to think about, much to do, and no time to waste.

On his way out he passed Michael, who had taken the opportunity to sneak back out to the front door and reclaim his boot, which still languished under Pretorius' shoe scraper. Shandor frowned, but said nothing.

Michael crept back into the dining room and stood discreetly in a corner. If Pretorius was in compliant mood he hoped to have another stab at extracting payment for the information about the sarcophagus. Beads of perspiration broke out on his brow as he studiously avoided Joachim's basilisk gaze.

Pretorius pricked Constance's forearm with a pin.

"It'll take more'an that to rouse her," ventured Michael. "She didn't bat an eyelid when I dropped her head on the cobbles."

The doctor straightened up and scratched his head.

"Fascinating," he mused, "but beyond my sphere of expertise. I am not primarily a medical practitioner. All I can surmise is that the young lady is in some sort of intense mesmeric trance."

"Is there nothing we can do?" Asked Talbot.

"I wish I knew," replied Pretorius. "You will have to consult a physician and alienist to learn any more."

"But where will I find such expertise in this desolate hole? There cannot be a specialist nearer than Prague."

"I beg to differ," said a cultivated voice from the doorway. "My name is Frankenstein. I am a doctor."

* * *

"Forgive me for letting myself in, Pretorius," said the Baron, "but the front door was open."

"Victor!" exclaimed the Doctor. "Come in, come in. Did you - er - pass the Father as you arrived?"

The Baron snorted.

"You need not fear for your reputation, old chap. I have no desire to reacquaint myself with that superstitious old goat. I kept to the shadows until he had waddled off."

The Baron turned his attentions toward the unconscious figure of Constance.

"So what seems to be ailing the young lady?" He asked. Pretorius introduced Talbot.

"It is an honour to meet you, Baron," said Talbot, eagerly taking Frankenstein's hand. "It was in the hope of arranging a consultation with you that I came to this neck of the woods."

"Flattered, I'm sure," replied Frankenstein, retrieving his hand as soon as politeness allowed. "But I am afraid that you have wasted your time. I make it a point of principle never to give consultations. I am involved in academic research only. This, however - " the Baron indicated the recumbent Constance " - is a different matter. It would be churlish of me to ignore an emergency; particularly when the victim is so charming."

Reminding himself that the Baron might be Connie's only chance of salvation, Talbot curbed the desire to punch him in the mouth. Instead, he embarked upon an explanation of the circumstances in which he had discovered his fiancé when a sudden realisation stopped him dead in mid-speech.

"Your nephew!" he exclaimed. "He is still up at the castle!"

"My nephew?" repeated the Baron. "What nephew, what castle? For goodness sake, do try to make sense, young man."

"Your nephew Ferdinand! He was to have made initial introductions between my fiancé and yourself. He went up to Castle Dracula - "

"Impudent puppy!" interrupted Frankenstein irritably. "And by what right does young Ferdinand think he can impose his cronies upon me without so much as a by-your-leave?"

Talbot finally lost the battle to rein in his anger.

"For God's sake, Baron, I am trying to tell you that your nephew is in mortal danger! Victoria - Ferdinand's fiancé - is already dead, murdered by the monsters which dwell in that damned place. Ajax, Constance's own brother, too: I was forced to wound him mortally. He had been...possessed."

"How tiresome," muttered the Baron. "I thought that the Count and I had reached an understanding. To be frank, I do not care two hoots about Ferdinand's fate - I scarcely know the boy, and what little I do know does not enamour me of him. But there are considerations of family to be taken into account; and then there is the principal of the thing. I must think about the course of action to be taken.

"May I suggest that I take your fiancé back to the castle tonight? Her cure may be a lengthy process, and I will need the resources of my laboratory.

"If you can cure my Connie, then we will follow you to the ends of the earth," replied Talbot.

Frankenstein had not meant his invitation to extend as far as the young man, but it was obvious that Talbot did not intend to let his fiancé out of his sight. Once he had them alone in the castle, the Baron thought, he would be able to separate them easily enough.

"Fortunately my humble dwelling is only a coach ride away," he said. "That is settled, then. In the mean time," he continued, turning to Pretorius, "I cannot see any reason why we should not continue with our plans for the evening?"

Overwhelmed by the tide of events, the Doctor shrugged his shoulders.

"I suppose not," he agreed wearily. "You will stay for dinner, Mr Talbot? You could freshen up while Joachim sorts you out some fresh clothes."

Talbot looked down at the recumbent form of his fiancé. The warmth of the library had brought some of the colour back to her cheeks, and her auburn hair tumbled over the cushions of the chaise longue. She looked as if she was merely sleeping. He nodded.

"Thank you, Doctor. I don't suppose another hour or so will make any difference, and what food the innkeeper was able to provide has barely touched my hunger. I could eat a horse."

"If you ate at the Crow and Gibbet then you have probably already done so," replied Pretorius. "I am sure that we can do better."

He instructed Joachim to set another place for dinner and was making his way across to the tantalus when he noticed Michael still lurking in the corner.

"Well?" he asked, fixing him with an acerbic eye. A drop of perspiration gathered at the end of Michael's nose and dripped onto the carpet.

"Begging your pardon Doctor, sir, and not wishing to be no bother and all, but I recalls you saying what you'd reyunermate me for finding that box. Sir. Begging your pardon."

Michael mumbled into silence and looked down at his boots. He could feel the doctor's eyes burning a hole into his bald patch as Pretorius wavered between honouring his contract and chucking Michael out on his ear.

Joachim returned and announced in fluent mime that a jug and basin awaited Talbot in the guest bedroom. A thrill of horror ran down whatever kept Michael upright in lieu of a spine. He was aware that Pretorius had only to say the word and Joachim would take pleasure in rending him limb from limb.

"Joachim, do we have any of the Turkish brandy left?"

Joachim nodded, and held up two fingers.

The Turkish brandy had been a mistake. Pretorius had seen it on special offer on a rare trip to Prague, and had bought a case on the principle that no brandy was undrinkable. One tasting had been enough to persuade him otherwise. The remaining eleven bottles had languished untouched in the cellar of the

Abbey house before Dominique had discovered that it was good for cleaning moss off the front steps.

"Nip down and get one for Michael, would you? I think it would make an appropriate reward for his contribution this afternoon. Hang on - why not give him both?"

Joachim grinned broadly and beckoned to Talbot and Michael. They followed him into the hall. Joachim left Michael waiting, and led the young man upstairs.

Michael rubbed his hands together in anticipation. Brandy! Two bottles! Perhaps Pretorius wasn't the bastard he had taken him for.

After a few minutes Joachim descended alone and disappeared down the hall, returning shortly with a pair of cobwebby bottles. He handed them to Michael with uncharacteristic good will, then opened the front door and ushered him out into the night.

* * *

Pretorius' dinner party had got off to a poor start, and didn't get much better. Even the warmth of Dominique's spicy cooking could not thaw the mutual frost that had formed between the Baron and Talbot, and Pretorius found himself struggling to keep the conversation from grinding to a halt.

He was further hampered by his own reluctance to discuss the one topic he knew Frankenstein wanted to raise. He managed to parry the Baron's first few openings, either by changing the subject, or by sending Joachim out to get some salt, or to fetch another bottle of wine from the cellar.

Eventually Frankenstein grew tired of the doctor's evasion and addressed him baldly.

"So tell me old chap," he said, wiping the corner of his mouth with his napkin, "are you going to win our little wager?"

Pretorius paused.

"My researches were going quite well until recently," he said.

"Unfortunately, I have been set back by the theft of an important research item - "

" - The Mummy?" interrupted Frankenstein. Very little got past the unwinking eye of Klove's telescope, and he dutifully reported to his master any activity in the village which he thought might be of interest.

Pretorius scowled.

" - The Mummy, yes. See here, Frankenstein, if you already knew that I had run into difficulties, then what damned point was there in asking me how I was doing?"

"Calm down, old chap," said the Baron in soothing tones, but with a tormenting gleam in his eye, "I had no intention of upsetting you. I was just making conversation."

"Is it impertinent of me to enquire as to the subject of this wager?" asked Talbot, genuinely interested in the conversation for the first time that evening. Frankenstein regarded him with cold disregard, and would have told him to mind his own business, had it not been for Pretorius' obvious embarrassment at the airing of the topic.

"Not at all," he said, with an affectedly casual air. "I have wagered the good doctor that I will discover the secret of life before he does."

"The secret of life?" Talbot repeated incredulously, "my God! And how do you intend to define success?"

"Quite simple," continued the Baron, "the stake goes to the first person who can successfully animate, or re-animate, dead flesh."

"But that is impossible!" gasped Talbot.

132

"Impossible? No. Difficult, certainly. Living entities - all living entities - are no more than machines. Immensely complicated machines, I'll grant you, but machines nonetheless - "

" - So you say!" interrupted Pretorius, finding his voice at last. He addressed Talbot.

"The Baron, you must appreciate, is an empiricist. It is his contention that every aspect of life can be reduced to the mechanical. There is no place in his philosophy for activity on any plane other than the physical. Thus he will always find his progress limited because he can never step out of the gutter. Whereas I - "

" - Whereas the doctor's head is in the clouds," broke in Frankenstein. "He would describe himself as a hermetic philosopher. I call him a muddle-nut. He fits out his laboratory with the trappings of scientific investigation, and spouts forth about his search for essences in terms which might convince a labourer's daughter: but strip away the window-dressing and he stands revealed in his pointed hat and apron, chanting incantations as he throws another toad into the cauldron."

Throughout Frankenstein's speech, Pretorius' face had been turning an ever deeper shade of purple. By the time the Baron paused to take a sip of wine he could no longer contain himself.

"And what are you? No more than a puppetmaker! Ha! But no matter how skilful your creations, and no matter what you may be able to give them the appearance of doing, all you will ever have at the end of the day is a bloody parody of life!"

What had started out twelve months ago as a harmless bet had come to symbolise the struggle for dominion between the Baron's philosophy and his own; a duel between science and alchemy, the physical and the metaphysical. And at present, the sad truth was that the metaphysical was losing hands down.

"Tell me," interceded Talbot, hoping to divert Pretorius' attention from the Baron's goading, "what is the stake in this titanic contest?"

"Stake? Five florins, and not a penny less," muttered Pretorius.

"Five florins?" repeated Talbot incredulously. "Five florins, for discovering the secrets of God? Why so derisory a sum?"

"And what would you propose?" snapped the doctor. "Fifty gold pieces? Five hundred? Five thousand? What value would you place upon the recreation of a soul?"

"Soul?" snorted Frankenstein. "Poppycock! Superstitious claptrap! Blood, bones and electricity, that is all."

And so the evening wore on. Talbot lapsed into silence, conscious that nothing he could say would distract the old rivals from their bickering. Furthermore, he was all too aware of the time passing by; and all the while Connie still lay comatose on the library couch.

Over the cheese the Baron casually let slip that he hoped to make an important announcement concerning his researches within the next fortnight. This plunged the doctor into a depression from which he did not emerge until Joachim was passing round the humidor.

Frankenstein, who had been pointedly ignoring Talbot's impatience through the last courses, helped himself to a second brandy before finally suggesting that his party should be making their way back to the castle. Talbot, much recovered and eager to be off, gathered Connie into his arms and followed Pretorius down the hall.

The doctor saw his guests out to the Baron's waiting coach-and-pair, and waited at the door while the hooded coachman clambered down from his seat to help Talbot load his fiancé aboard. Talbot thanked Pretorius for his kindness, and climbed in after her. Frankenstein and the doctor exchanged farewells with reasonably convincing good grace, then the Baron tapped on the ceiling of the coach with his cane. The coachman cracked his whip and the horses broke trotted off down the drive.

Pretorius waited at the door, bathed in the orange glow of the hall lamp, looking after the coach until it disappeared into the night. He wished he could believe that the young couple's ordeal was at an end, and that things were going to get better for them from now on: but lurking deep within him was a nagging suspicion that their troubles were only just beginning.

Chapter 14

Ripper glanced across to the passenger seat and grinned. Roy Stewart looked like a sardine must do from the inside of the tin. He had slumped down in his seat in order not to press his head against the roof, but as a consequence, his knees were now up around his ears.

He might have been more comfortable in Ripper's little 1963 MG convertible had they been able to take the top down, but it was a gloomy and cold evening, with a light drizzle that the wipers were busily sweeping off the windscreen.

Ripper was giving the actor playing Joachim a lift back to London. Ripper lived in Oxfordshire, but was heading to the West End for the evening to attend the premier of a play in which one of his old friends from rep days was performing.

He and Stewart had never acted together – or even met - before this film, and the car ride was the first opportunity for them to exchange anything more than daily pleasantries and their lines.

"Joan told me you own a gymnasium in town," said Ripper. 'Joan' was Joan Sims – the film's Elsbieta - who always knew everything about everybody, including some things some actors might rather had not been known by anyone.

"I do." Said Stewart with evident pride. "That's where I'm heading this evening. It's the first mixed-race gymnasium in England."

"You're kidding me!"

"As God's my witness! There's a couple more now, but when I set it up back in fifty-four, it was the first."

"Was that what you did in Jamaica before you came over? Ran a gym?"

Stewart smiled and shook his head. "Far from it. I was a scrawny young man. No, my ambition was to be a doctor. That was what I came over here to do. But - well, you know - some things are more difficult for a black man."

"So how did you get into acting?" asked Ripper.

"It was just a happy accident. An actor friend of mine – a white man - auditioned for a play that had a black character role. The director asked him if he knew any black actors. He gave my name, then rang me up and told me I'd become an actor. So I auditioned, got the part and enjoyed it. Best of all, I got paid for it - and at that time I really needed the money. After that: you know how it is, you get the bug.

"I did a few plays, then started to go for small roles in movies. Nothing much: African natives, slaves, tribal chiefs if I was lucky. But I kept seeing white stuntmen blacking up to do the action scenes, and I realised that there was a gap in the market.

"So I made up my mind to become the first black stuntman in Britain. To do that, I needed to get into shape and learn how to fight and take a fall. But no white gym would consider admitting a black man, and there were no black gyms – leastways, none where I cared to spend any amount of time –so I realised the only way I was going to be able to train was to open my own. And that's what I did."

"I really admire that," said Ripper, "Not letting anything stand in your way. You know, I was having a whinge the other day about being typecast as the drunken derelict who gets killed by the monster every time; but I really ought to count my blessings. It must be so much more difficult to be constantly dressed up in grass skirts and bone necklaces. Don't you ever get fed up of it?"

Stewart gave a rather Gallic shrug.

"Of course I'd be delighted if the RSC rang me up to play Othello, but until the day they do, I'll deliver the lines - or in Joachim's case, the grunts - and take the money. Jack Mandora mi no choose none."

"Jack who? Asked Ripper, taking his eyes off the road for a moment.

Stewart laughed. "Jack Mandora mi no choose none", he repeated. It's what my mama used to say at the end of every Anansi story. You know Anansi?"

Ripper shook his head. "Never heard of it."

"Anansi is a spider. There are lots of stories about him in Jamaica. Sometimes he's cunning and tricks people, other times he's greedy or stupid and gets punished. But every story ends with the storyteller saying, 'Jack Mandora mi no choose none'. It means something like, 'I've repeated the story exactly as I was told it'.

"'I haven't changed a word'?" suggested Ripper.

"Exactly. I read in The Gleaner – that's the Jamaican newspaper my brother sometimes sends me - that the Anansi stories originated in Africa and came over to Jamaica in the slave ships and were passed down through the generations by word of mouth. So I guess it was important that the words were preserved as they were retold.

"But 'Jack Mandora mi no choose none' means something more than that. It's a kind of disclaimer: it's also saying – how do the newspapers' letters pages put it? 'I assume no responsibility for the views expressed in this story'.

"So when Mama told me a story where Anansi did something bad and ended it by saying 'Jack Mandora mi no choose none' she was also letting me know that she was not giving me permission to copy his bad behaviour and that if I did, I could expect a licking."

As Stewart mined back into the seam of his memories, Ripper noticed that his Jamaican accent came more to the fore.

"It's a useful phrase," he said, "I wish I could pretend I was going to remember it tomorrow, because I could imagine myself using it. It would sometimes be useful to be able to disclaim responsibility for my lines."

Stewart smiled. "True brother: sometimes you just have to get the job done and get out," he said. "I've just finished my scenes in a movie by some idiot French director who was clearly just making it up as he went along."

"What was your part?"

Stewart laughed. "Hard to tell," he said. "I seemed to be a member of a black power revolutionary cell, operating out of a scrapyard in Battersea. But then some women in white dresses turned up and we painted them red."

"I beg your pardon?" exclaimed Ripper.

"The director gave us red paint and brushes and we had to daub them with red paint. Then they laid down on cars.

"Apparently it's going to have a soundtrack by the Rolling Stones, though, so who knows? Maybe it will do okay with the art house crowd. But it's not going to be remembered as a cinematic masterpiece, and with any due respect, Monsieur Jean-Luc Godard is not the genius he'd like to think he is."

"Never heard of him," said Ripper.

Chapter 15

Talbot had been here before. The stone flags, cold and greasy beneath his running feet; the oppressive gloom, broken only by the ghostly presence of the vaulted columns; and the echo of water dripping from some far-off crack in the ceiling; all these things seemed familiar, but somehow strange.

He was searching desperately, but for whom or for what he had no idea. He peered ahead into the darkness and to either side, straining to recognise any landmark that might tell him where he was or what he was doing here.

Suddenly a swathe of scarlet satin opened up in front of him. In the middle of the crimson sheet a demonic face hung suspended, like some loathsome spider waiting in its web for its next victim. The jaundiced and haggard features of that face were engraved with centuries of unimaginable depravity and appalling horrors. Its jaws opened wide, revealing the yellowed and crooked fangs of some ancient beast.

Unable to check his pace, Talbot hurtled headlong into the cape and tumbled to the ground, entangled in its folds. He tore at the cloth, expecting at any moment to feel the monster's breath upon his neck, and the touch of those deadly incisors. But the more he struggled, the tighter he wrapped himself in the suffocating fabric.

Then it ripped, and Talbot found himself looking through his torn sheets at Baron Frankenstein, who made no effort to conceal his amusement.

"Good morning," said the Baron. "I will ask Klove to provide you with stronger linen tonight."

Talbot clawed his way out of the torn and sweat-sodden bed sheets and threw them aside. He sat up in bed, still trembling.

"My apologies," he said stiffly, embarrassed and annoyed that the Baron had entered his room without knocking. "Just a nightmare. I will pay for the damage, of course."

Frankenstein waved away the suggestion.

"I have brought water," he said, indicating a blue and white jug from which wisps of steam were rising. "I live alone, with only one servant, the present whereabouts of whom I am at a loss to know. Breakfast awaits in the morning room."

"How is - ?"

But before Talbot was able to enquire after his fiancé's condition the Baron had left the room, closing the door silently behind him.

* * *

Frankenstein walked down the corridor, towards Miss Quigley's chamber. As he approached he was surprised to see that her door was ajar. He tiptoed the last few yards and peered through the crack.

The young woman lay exactly as the men had left her last night, with her flame-red hair spilling over the pillow and her head tilted slightly towards the door. Despite his obvious exhaustion Talbot had insisted on putting her to bed himself, and would have slept in the chair beside her had Frankenstein not been at pains to persuade him that he, too, was in need of a good night's sleep. The Baron was rapidly losing patience with the young American; his headstrong attitude might well prove to be a nuisance if it came into conflict with the Baron's own aims, as seemed inevitable.

As Frankenstein edged closer to the door and gained a wider view, his nostrils flared in aristocratic ire. Klove was in the room, sitting on the edge of the bed, gazing open-mouthed at the serene features of its occupant.

142

Frankenstein pushed the door open. Klove leapt to his feet, his cheeks flushed with embarrassment.

"Ah, there you are, Klove," said the Baron pleasantly, "please don't get up on my account."

Klove started to babble an incoherent apology, but Frankenstein waved him down.

"Not at all, my dear boy. I understand - you were just having a little rest? Tut, tut! I must work you too hard. Perhaps you would be happier in somebody else's employ?"

Klove's protestations redoubled. The Baron continued.

"Or perhaps it is your medication? I have often noticed how lethargic it makes you. Maybe we should withhold it for a few days, just to make sure that it is not doing you any harm, eh?"

"Oh no, Master, please, not that!" pleaded Klove, wringing his hands in supplication. He dropped to the floor and approached Frankenstein on his knees.

"I'll never do it again, never! I promise you, Master," he whined, plucking at the Baron's sleeve.

Frankenstein drew back his hand and delivered Klove a blow that knocked him across the room and into the dresser.

"How dare you touch me!" he hissed, striding across to the cowering servant and dragging him to his feet by the collar. "And don't think that I didn't see you leering at Miss Quigley. My God! The very idea! Do you think that any woman would look twice at a pathetic worm like you? Well, do you?"

"No, Master," replied Klove miserably. Frankenstein pushed him towards the door.

"Go to the laboratory. Make it ready for me and wait there," he commanded. "Now get out of my sight!"

Klove limped out of the room. A few moments later Frankenstein derived cruel satisfaction from the sound of sobbing in the corridor. He closed the door.

Alone with her at last! He had been anticipating this moment since he had first seen Constance lying helpless and vulnerable on Pretorius' chaise longue.

He sat down on the edge of the bed and inspected her face. She was flawless! Her complexion was as smooth as cream, her cheeks rose-tinted and her full red lips seemed to yearn for the kiss of a knowledgeable man. He reached over and arranged a lock of her auburn hair on the pillow with trembling fingers. Emboldened by this first contact he traced the delicate outline of her ear, then brushed her cheek with his fingertips.

Not for Victor, seventh Baron Frankenstein, a life dedicated entirely to academic pursuits, like some secular monk! No, he was as red blooded as any man, indeed, more so than most; for through the liberating power of his intellect he had travelled beyond the self-imposed limits of ordinary desire to explore the dark regions beyond.

In his student days he had come close to expulsion when some damned publican's daughter had gone home wailing to her father and shown him the weals upon her back. It had taken all his powers of persuasion and a great deal of money to silence them, and he had suffered the humiliation of being gated for the rest of the term.

But the young Frankenstein's objects of desire had been limited by what money could buy. With his unlimited means he could - and did - procure any number of boozy serving wenches and raddled whores upon whom to expiate his cruel lust, but eventually their very availability led him to despise them. He found little pleasure in the infliction of pain and humiliation on those pathetic creatures who had never known anything but degradation throughout their sad lives.

How much more meaningful would be the act and by consequence how much sweeter the pleasure if it was to be inflicted upon one who had never known real suffering before!

Thus, Frankenstein had turned his attentions towards the young and innocent daughters of Ingolstadt's better born families. But his unsavoury reputation went before him, and even in those cases where it did not, all his charm could not counter the instinctive revulsion he engendered in his would-be victims. Over twelve months of trying, he had endured hundreds of cups of tea and thousands of hours of tedious conversation, and still had not managed to separate a single daughter from her chaperone for so much as a half-hour. In frustration he had damned the lot of them and returned to his former haunts.

In his twentieth year the direction that his academic researches were taking had been brought to the attention of the college authorities, and their patience finally came to an end.

He had fled Ingolstadt and returned to Karnstein to claim the family seat. The isolated castle had proven an ideal laboratory for him to continue with his experiments, while the deference of the peasantry had allowed him to indulge his depraved appetites without too much scandal.

But even in the fastness of the castle which bore his family name he was not safe from the prying eyes and wagging tongues of the superstitious and small minded. Reports of disinterred corpses, and of a laboratory that resembled a charnel-house more than a temple of learning, reached the ears of the zealous Father Shandor.

With a deputation including the Burgomeister, the priest had forced his way into the castle and asked a lot of damn fool questions. After muttering darkly about desecration and blasphemy, they had given Frankenstein an ultimatum: either he quit his researches, or face the wrath of the village. By way of an answer, Frankenstein had ordered his staff to throw the party out. When they refused, he had seized a poker and set about the lot of them, Priest, Burgomeister, servants and all.

That night he had suffered the ultimate humiliation of being hounded from his own property by a torch-wielding mob. He had been obliged to flee through one of the castle's several secret entrances, and had watched, hidden at a safe distance, as they ransacked the buildings and finally put the place to the torch. As smoke rose into the night sky he had turned his back on his ancestral home, vowing never to return.

He had roamed Europe for six years, setting up his laboratory wherever he found himself, adding to his knowledge little by little, but constantly frustrated by the interference of the authorities and by the need to move on.

At last, pragmatism had overcome his principles, and one winter's night he had returned on horseback to the burnt-out shell of Castle Frankenstein. It was obvious from the wild dereliction that nobody had visited the castle since the night the mob had attacked. Half an hour of tearing away brambles and throwing aside blackened and rotten beams had revealed a trap door still intact. Forcing the trap open, he had discovered that a whole suite of cellars had survived the conflagration. That night he had slept below ground with his only cloak around him for warmth.

The next day he had ridden away again to a distant town, beyond the range of gossip, and had returned with builders and carpenters hired at twice the standard rate in return for oaths of discretion. They had been followed by a seemingly endless succession of ox carts laden with materials brought across the mountains at breathtaking expense.

Over many months the castle had been rebuilt from the cellars up. The Baron had taken great pains to ensure that none of the restoration was visible from the village, which considerably reduced the number of rooms that could be restored. But he had no plans to engage servants this time - he had not forgotten his previous betrayal.

The last delivery had been made by a string of packhorses. As soon as they had finished unloading the animals, Frankenstein had paid off the drivers and dismissed all the craftsmen.

Alone at last, he had unpacked the baskets, carefully removing layers of straw to uncover the delicate glass retorts, the bottles and jars of chemicals, and the electrical apparatus with which he was to equip his laboratory.

Self-contained and undisturbed, his modest needs provided for by a monthly trip to a far-flung town, Frankenstein had embarked once again on his research. This time, progress was swift; so swift that before long he found his demand for animals upon which to perform his experiments outstripping the supply. He returned from his next trip to town with a variety of traps and gins that he set up on the mountainside around the castle. It had been during one of his rounds of inspection that he had found Klove, unconscious and close to death. The rest of the story had been the history of Klove's ruination.

There is a tide in the life of man, thought the Baron, which if taken at the flood...

With Klove, he had seized the chance to delegate the last few irritating domestic duties distracting him from his work. Now, fate had presented him with the opportunity to his live out his Sadean fantasies upon the voluptuous form of Constance Quigley. Fate was not going to find him backward.

His fingertips trailed down her cheek to brush her lips, and meandered down her smooth throat until their progress was impeded by the bedclothes that Talbot had tucked prudishly around her shoulders. Frankenstein's fingers grasped the edge of the sheet.

The sound of footsteps in the corridor outside made him let go and rise, hastily, to his feet. A few seconds later Talbot walked in, dressed and with his wounded arm cradled in a makeshift sling. He looked at the Baron suspiciously.

"No change in our patient this morning," said Frankenstein breezily. "Never mind. We will embark on her treatment later this morning."

"What are you proposing to do?" asked Talbot.

Nothing that offers the slightest risk of waking her up, thought Frankenstein; at least, not until you are out of the way.

"We will start on a course of stimulant drugs, and proceed from there. I am going to my laboratory to prepare them now. In the mean time, you must be hungry. Let me accompany you to the morning room."

Without giving Talbot a moment to protest, the Baron led him out of the room and back down the hall.

* * *

Although Baron Frankenstein had been obliged to build his laboratory in the cellars, it was a spacious and high-ceilinged room nonetheless. It had been fitted out and equipped with every convenience and piece of scientific gadgetry imaginable. A broad oak worktop ran around three of the walls, fitted below with cupboards and sets of drawers.

Along the length of the worktop was laid out a bewildering variety of apparatus. Here, a spirit lamp kept a purple fluid bubbling in its retort, forcing tinted steam through a bewildering maze of tubes and condensers: there, a plaster and wax anatomical model peeled away successive layers of a human head.

The fourth wall was covered with shelf upon shelf of academic books and journals: a set of library steps was on hand to help reach the upper shelves. A chain hoist, currently not in use, hung down from a gantry on the roof.

Although his tears had dried, Klove still sniffed occasionally as he swept the floor. It was not the Baron's act of ritual humiliation that had affected him so deeply - he was used to that - nor even the threat to withhold his morphine. What had cast him into the pit of despair, as always, was his own participation in his degradation.

Every time he felt the pangs of addiction clawing at his stomach, or heard himself grovelling to the man he hated more than any other; whenever he saw his own hands holding down some poor shrieking beast while the Baron embarked upon yet another cruel experiment, he was confronted with what he had become, and he despised himself for it.

When his spirit was at its lowest ebb, he could convince himself that his whole destiny was blighted. In black misery he would trace his ill-fortune back to his very conception, to the terrible legacy his mother had only dared to reveal to him when he had become a man. On rare occasions, however, he found the inner strength to fight the influence of malign exterior forces and his own weakness.

Last night he had seen a vision, a vision of everything that he was not. As he had helped Talbot lift Miss Quigley down from the carriage and carry her to her bedroom, Klove had been captivated by her beauty and her radiant innocence.

He had spent a sleepless night tossing and turning, unwilling and unable to erase her image from his mind's eye. He had risen early and gone to her chamber to sit at the foot of her bed and watch the dawn's wan light break over her ivory perfection.

Frankenstein's taunts about Miss Quigley's unavailability had not stung Klove as the Baron had intended them to, for the manservant already regarded her as completely beyond his reach, as far above him as the stars are from the gutter. His conscience had been troubled even by his own presumption in watching her as she slept; notions of any more intimate contact, had they crossed his mind, would have shocked him as a sacrilege.

He collected the floor sweepings into a shovel and tipped them into the bin. He was well aware that no matter how thoroughly he executed his duties this morning, the Baron was bound to find fault with his work; but he held out a faint hope that if he was assiduous enough he might escape without a beating.

He parked the broom in a corner and walked over to the two trolleys that stood side-by-side in the middle of the laboratory floor.

Both were covered with sheets. Under one lay the grotesque assemblage of human remains which the Baron, in his madness, believed that he would soon imbue with the spark of life. Its bandaged feet stuck out from beneath the sheet.

The sheet over the other trolley was sodden with blood. Klove stripped it off, rolled it into a ball and flung it in a corner, revealing the corpse that Klove had stolen from the joiner's workshop two nights ago. It was naked now, more naked than ever it had been in life: the Baron had slit its belly open from rib cage to crotch and across from side to side. Clamps held back the flaps of skin, revealing the mauled organs and glistening viscera. One arm ended in a stump at the wrist. The missing hand now adorned the abomination on the other trolley. A large glass bottle hung inverted from a stand by the side of the trolley. Clear tubes lead from the neck of the bottle and entered the corpse through incisions in the neck. Klove could see blood moving sluggishly through the tubes, feeding the delicate tissues of the brain.

Yesterday the Baron had cut the top off the carter's skull and poked around a bit. Today the Baron intended to transfer the brain to the empty skull of his creation. The skull cap had been tied back in place, protecting the contents until this morning's operation.

Klove leant over and plucked at a loose thread protruding from under the corpse's chin. Too late he realised that it was not a thread at all, but the ragged end of the cord which bound the top of the head in place. Its jaw dropped open; so did Klove's. The bloody skull cap dropped off the end of the trolley and fell on to the floor. Klove bent down to pick it up.

He saw the brain slithering out of the cranial cavity from the corner of his eye and made a wild grab for it, but slipped the puddle of blood that had gathered under the corpse. He crashed into the apparatus beside the trolley. The stand toppled over, pulling the tubes out of the corpse's neck and crashed to the ground. The bottle exploded into a thousand pieces, showering Klove with blood and broken glass. The brain hit the floor with a squelch.

Klove stared in speechless horror at the grey jelly spattered across the flags, then fell to his knees and started scooping it up in his hands and trying to stuff it back into the carter's skull.

"You bloody fool! Do you know what you have done?"

Klove looked up. The Baron stood at the top of the stairs, white-faced and shaking with rage. He strode down the stairs and across the laboratory to the bench, picked up a short length of rubber tubing and advanced towards his cowering servant.

Chapter 16

Dawn broke gently over Karnstein, as if in deference to the quantities of alcohol that had been consumed throughout the village the night before. Mist softened the brightness of the morning sun.

Michael awoke slowly, the layers of his dreams being stripped away one by one like dirty bedsheets on washing day. He lay awake, silent and still, at peace with the world and with himself. No hangover! Not even a twinge. That was the mark of a good drop, that was.

He wondered why he was in a box.

It was a nice enough box in itself, to be sure; roomy and faintly scented with pine resin, though damper than he might have wished. He lay stretched out full length in it, staring up at the rafters supporting a low roof. Here and there, daylight shone through the gaps between the slates.

It occurred to him that he might have died in the night, and that he was now laid out in his coffin awaiting interment. That could explain the absence of a hangover.

He sat up and looked around. It was not, to his relief, the joiner's Chapel of Rest but another, unfamiliar outhouse. Boxes and tea chests were piled up all around him, rusty garden implements hung from hooks on the walls, and strange mechanical devices gathered dust. Daylight filtered in through the cracked panes of a small window.

Lying on its side near the crate was an empty bottle. Michael picked it up and cradled it fondly in the palm of his hand. He inspected the label, admiring the wiggly script and its brightly coloured illustration of a belly dancer, then put the open mouth to his eye like a telescope and peered inside. A single drop trickled down the neck and into his eye. He cursed. It could not have been more painful had he jabbed himself with a flaming brand. He rolled the weeping eyeball around in its socket and blinked away his tears.

Clambering out of the crate he inadvertently planted his foot in a puddle of vomit. It was the smallest of several similar puddles that decorated the floor, the walls and, in what must have been a spectacularly athletic act, the ceiling.

"Sweet Mary's titties! Them Turkeys certainly knows how to make brandy," he exclaimed in admiration.

From the outside, he recognised the crate as the box from Eejit, the one that the late carter had been delivering to the Doctor and which Joachim had pulled out of the Farkle. With an almost audible grinding of mental wheels he deduced that he had not managed to get any further than an outbuilding of the Abbey House the previous evening. Stepping daintily over his puke he made his way across to the tiny window and rubbed the grime off the pane with his cuff.

Sure enough, there was Joachim, crossing a wide, ill-kempt lawn with a bucket of water in each hand. Michael ducked down low until the manservant had disappeared round far the side of the house.

There was no point in hanging around, he thought to himself; not with the butler of Satan about. He would just retrieve the other bottle and be on his way. He looked round for it.

One of Michael's worst habits, in Michael's opinion, was that of concealing his drink. On the rare occasions when he was too drunk to finish a bottle at night, a paranoid fear would possess him that it might be stolen while he slept. In order to prevent that appalling possibility he would stumble about for ages, looking for the perfect place to conceal the bottle. Whether or not this worked,

Michael was unable to say, as he had never yet been able to recall his hiding place the following morning.

He rummaged through the boxes beside the crate, at first carefully, trying not to disturb the order of the contents. As the enormity of his loss bore down on him, however, he grew frantic, clawing the contents out in handfuls and finally emptying the boxes over the floor.

At last, he had to admit defeat and slumped forlornly to the floor, clasping the empty bottle to his chest like a child comforting herself with her doll.

When a decent period of mourning had elapsed, prudence dug him in the ribs and reminded him that he was still in enemy territory. He stood the bottle on a tea chest to remain as a monument to his achievement in finishing it – and to irritate Joachim when he eventually came upon it - and rose to his feet. After a brief reconnaissance through the window to make sure that the coast was still clear, he opened the door and slipped out.

* * *

Wednesday was market day, so Michael set off towards town. By the time he reached the village a handful of stalls had already set up on the green opposite the Crow and Gibbet. The market was busier than usual, with villagers gathering in small groups to exchange their versions of the events of the last four days. A topic of particular scrutiny was young Talbot's account of his encounter with vampires up at Castle Dracula. Gimmer Schwab claimed to have lived through three infestations and nobody else in the village was old enough to contradict him.

" - Course, 'forty-two twarn't as bad as 'twenty-six. Now, 'twenty-six, that was a bugger of a year. Scores dead - and undead, mark you. Twarn't just the vampires, neither; there was the Reptile an' all."

"The Reptile?" repeated Maude Bumblewicz, at once enthralled and horrified.

"You mean you ain't heard on the Reptile, Maudy girl? Oh dear, oh lor', these young 'uns don't know as they're born.

"Harrible the Reptile was, all covered in scales an' that. Did for a good few while it lasted! It had fangs, see, a'drip with venom. One bite and you swelled right up. I see'd Tom's father, Old Tom, just after he'd been bit. His face had turned black as an old 'tater and the foam was pouring out of his mouth like I don't know what. I don't reckon as I'll ever forget the pitiful noises he was making, screamin' and gurglin' his last few breaths away."

Maude buried her face in her mother's skirts.

On the far side of the green a curious restructuring of the social politics of the village womenfolk was taking place. Intrigued by the garbled fragments of Talbot's story they had received between the pants and groans of last night's late customers, Elsbieta and a couple of her workmates from the Lair had risen early and drifted over to the market to catch up on events.

Despite her advancing years - she was in her fifties - Elsbieta still worked in the brothel. Losing her son had pitched her back into the cosy womb of the Lair for support, and there, safe within its plush-lined walls, she had stayed. Unlike the other women, Elsbieta made no attempt to conceal her age by raddling her cheeks or adopting girlish affectations. Whilst her services were not in the greatest demand, she nonetheless maintained a regular clientele who came to her for companionship and good conversation as much as for physical comfort.

Hated by the wives of the village, who were aware that the girls were on far more intimate terms with their most of their husbands than they were themselves, and despised by the unmarried girls for their moral laxity, Elsbieta and her friends were used to getting the cold-shoulder in any gathering. Thus it was no surprise to them when none of the women huddled together in conversation acknowledged their approach.

By dint of having worked in service in Prague as a girl, Kitty, the Smith's wife held herself and was generally regarded as worldly wise. From this position she was holding forth.

"They say that when he feeds, his victims are overcome with voluptuous pleasure."

The older women clucked darkly and shook their heads.

"But with that first unholy kiss, the beast infects them with its own foul appetites. They become licentious and depraved -"

"- There's some as I can think of who'd scarce notice any difference," sniffed Granny Blepp, folding her arms across her bosom and directing a sidelong glance towards Elsbieta.

"Of course," continued Kitty Smith, "he prefers virgins."

Now it was the turn of the younger women to react. All of a sudden the moral high ground didn't feel like quite the safe territory they had always assumed it to be. Elsbieta whispered something to her friends, and all three of them collapsed into a fit of giggles. Several virgins of various vintages glared at the whores, their expressions tinged for the first time with jealousy.

Despite the crowds, business on the market was slack. Only Goodwife Brockhaus' vegetable stall was busy. Anticipating market trends, Brockhaus' family had risen early and spent the hours before dawn in the vegetable patch. Blithely ignoring the grumbles of the townsfolk at the outrageous prices she was asking, the Goodwife was doing a roaring trade in garlic.

Paying little attention to the hubbub of the market place, Michael ambled about the stalls with his eyes fixed firmly on the ground. Every now and then he bent down to recover a fallen vegetable or a worm-eaten piece of fruit. Before long his pockets were bulging with the makings of a substantial if unappetising meal. Leaving the bustle of the market behind him, he headed off towards the churchyard in search of a peaceful spot to eat breakfast.

* * *

When Widow Mordant walked into the study she found Father Shandor slumped across the desk, fast asleep. Piled up around him and strewn across the floor were ancient volumes on supernatural lore. By his side stood an empty brandy bottle and a tumbler. The Widow pursed her lips.

When Shandor had fallen prey to drink all those years ago, it had been Widow Mordant who had finally confronted him, and it was she who had stood by him through his battle to conquer his addiction. Since then she had kept watch over him with an eagle eye, and had scolded him thoroughly at the first suggestion of a relapse. This was not the time, however.

She picked up the glass and bottle and tiptoed out of the room, coming back a minute later with a blanket, which she draped over the old man's shoulders.

An hour and a half later she entered the room again bearing a covered tray. She placed the tray on the desk in front of the priest and shook him gently by the shoulder. He awoke with a start.

"Wh-what time is it?" he mumbled, rubbing his eyes.

"It's gone eight, Father."

Shandor began to rise.

"I must speak with the Burgomeister. There is not a moment to lose."

Widow Mordant gently restrained him.

"If you intend to argue with that puffed up old fool, forgive me Father but I speak as I find, then you'll be needing a decent breakfast inside you."

158

Obediently, Shandor sat back down. Before the Widow withdrew her hand from his shoulder he laid his own hand briefly over hers.

"You're a good woman, Agnes," he said.

A trained eye might have detected a momentary twitch at the corners of the Widow's lips.

"Very kind of you to say so, Father, I'm sure. Don't let your sausage get cold."

* * *

After breakfast Father Shandor donned his cloak and left the Presbytery, clutching a bundle of the books he had been studying all night. In the churchyard he passed Michael, who was scuttling along the path with the single-minded intensity of a dung beetle on the trail of a fresh deposit. Shandor was too preoccupied to enquire the nature of Michael's business, though he had no doubt that it was something of which he would disapprove, had he time to do so. They exchanged the most perfunctory of greetings and continued on their separate ways.

As Shandor neared the Manor House the dogs gave warning of his approach, and by the time he walked through the gates the Burgomeister was already standing in the doorway in his dressing gown, with a slice of toast in his hand.

His wrathful expression did not augur well for the Father.

"Shandor!" he exclaimed with his mouth full. "You have saved my men a trip. I was just about to instruct them to arrest you."

Shandor glowered at him.

"Arrest me? I'd like to see you try! And why, may I ask would you want to arrest a man of the cloth?"

"It seems to me that I have quite a range of offences to choose from, Father. What about aiding and abetting an escaped criminal, to start with?"

Shandor was not in the least surprised that von Trapp had already heard about Talbot's dramatic reappearance, nor that the Burgomeister was aware of the Father's own part in caring for him. News travelled through the Vale of Walach faster than the Farkle, and von Trapp had his own spies in the village.

"Criminal? Don't be absurd! Talbot may suffer from periodic fits of madness, but he is no criminal. What should concern you is the story he had to tell - "

"How dare you presume to tell me what should or should not be my concern!" boomed von Trapp. "You may choose to believe the word of a lunatic - "

"Lord, give me strength!" muttered Shandor through clenched teeth. "What more evidence do you need before you start to take this horror seriously? People are dying! Aye, that and worse!

"For God's sake, Burgomeister, I was damn near killed by poor Philomena Blepp, God rest her soul, two days after we laid her body to rest!"

Throughout the course of Shandor's tirade, the Burgomeister's colour had been fading from a congested purple which had pleasantly complemented the mauve of his dressing gown to a jaundiced yellowy-grey which clashed abominably.

When he spoke again he was unable to recapture the note of righteous indignation he had been employing hitherto.

"But Dracula was put to death years ago! You and I both stood side by side and watched him turn to dust before our eyes!"

"I have seen many things, Burgomeister; enough to know that evil never dies completely - "

"- And what if he has found a way to return?" interrupted Von Trapp. "Just supposing - and I am not for a moment acknowledging that possibility, except for the sake of argument - but supposing he has, what do you expect to do about it?"

"He has not been back long. For the moment he will be weak. We must strike now, before he regains his full strength; before he can protect himself with an army of his own kind.

"We must summon together a party to go up to the Castle. We can go during daylight hours, when he is sleeping."

"And how do you propose that we kill him this time, eh, Father?"

Shandor's heart sank. For a moment he had thought that he had been making progress. But from the sneer in Von Trapp's voice he could tell that the idiot had retreated into the shelter of his own pomposity. Still, he come got too far to give up now.

"There are ways," he said, patting his parcel, "set out in these books. More ways than you might have thought. It will not be easy, Burgomeister, but we have destroyed him before. There is no reason why we cannot do it again."

Shandor fell silent. There was nothing left in him to say. He stared unblinking at the Burgomeister, who was unable to return his gaze. His eyes darted about like birds in a cage. At last he spoke.

"I must consider this further," he declared. "There is no good to be done and a great deal of harm in creating alarm in the village without good reason - No!" he held up his hand, silencing Shandor's exclamation of protest. "That is my final word. I will give you my decision tomorrow. In the mean time, if it reaches my ears that you or anybody else is attempting to act without my authority, I will have no alternative but to order your arrest.

"Now, I am afraid that I can give you no more of my time. I have work to do."

With that he turned on his heel and disappeared back into the Manor, slamming the door behind him.

Chapter 17

Pretorius sat at the breakfast table in his dressing gown, staring at the cataracted eye of his fried egg with little enthusiasm.

After he had seen off his dinner guests last night he had returned to the library for a last brandy. In a vain attempt to drown his humiliation and to silence the insidious whisper of his conscience, he had continued to refill his glass until he fell asleep. When Joachim had come in to lock up for the night, he had found the Doctor unconscious in his chair, a half-empty glass hanging precariously between limp fingers. Joachim had picked him up as easily and as lovingly as if he had been a sleeping child and carried him up to bed.

Pretorius had woken several times in the night and finally rose early, still weary but unable to sleep any longer. He felt like death, and looked like it too. He pushed his plate away.

Dominique came in with another pot of coffee. She refilled the doctor's cup and waited. Pretorius clutched the cup between trembling hands, raised it to his lips and drank too fast, scalding the roof of his mouth. When the tears cleared from his eyes he noticed that Dominique was still standing beside him. He raised an eyebrow to her.

She approached the table, nervously wringing the corner of her apron.

"Can I speak with you, doctor?" she asked.

Pretorius was by no means in a mood for social intercourse; nonetheless he pulled himself up in his chair, rubbed his eyes and did his best to look attentive.

"How can I help you, dear?" he asked.

Dominique paused for a moment, formulating her line of approach.

"Joachim told me that you quarrelled with Frankenstein last night - please don't think that he betrayed your confidence. He knows that I would not speak of it beyond these walls - "

Pretorius managed a wan smile.

"It never ceases to amaze me how much Joachim manages to tell you without words. As to any indiscretion, please do not apologise, my dear. I would be offended to think that I was not the subject of conversation once in a while."

"He said that the two of you had made a wager - a wager which concerned life... and death."

"In a manner of speaking," said Pretorius cautiously. It occurred to him that Dominique and Joachim might find his field of investigation antithetical to their own spiritual beliefs, whatever they were. Curious, he thought, that he had never bothered to ask them. Pretorius knew that he would rather abandon the bet and lose what little dignity he had, than offend his two friends.

"He gave me to understand that you were competing to create life from dead flesh."

Pretorius gave a shrug which turned itself into a nod without his consent.

"Joachim gained the impression that winning this wager mattered to you a great deal. He also believes that you are not doing as well you had hoped, and that you fear the Baron will succeed in his quest before you."

Pretorius sighed.

"Joachim is correct in every respect," he said wearily. "It must seem like the most appalling vanity to you. But the wager itself is not the thing - "

"Oh, no doctor, you misunderstand. I have not come to complain: I have a proposal to make."

Pretorius was intrigued. He pulled himself up in his chair.

"Go on," he said.

"For some time now, Joachim and I have had enough money saved up to consider embarking on the last stage of our journey home. We knew that you would not refuse us permission to leave your service, but we felt - we feel - that we are still under a great obligation to you. You saved my life, and you offered us your support when we were alone and helpless. I believe that I may have found a way to repay you for your kindness.

"You have heard, I think, that some credit me with supernatural powers. Whether you listen to those stories I do not know. You are a wise man, doctor; too wise to be taken in by mere superstition, but wise enough to keep an open mind. So all I ask is that you allow me to demonstrate that I can do precisely what it is you are seeking to do - "

" - I'm sorry, Dominique," interrupted Pretorius. "I am not sure that I follow you."

" What I am saying, Doctor, is that I can show you how to restore life - of a sort - to the dead!"

"What? But how? How can you know that which I - which the Baron - ?"

"I make no claim to any great personal wisdom, doctor. Everything I know was passed down to me by my mother. That knowledge she had learned on her own mother's knee before me, and so on back through countless generations. It is the wisdom, not of one great man, but of many wise women.

"To our forebears, it was Ju Ju. The enslaved generation named it Voodoo. For those of us who practise it, it has a secret name that may not be revealed.

"The knowledge you desire, the revival of the dead, we call Zombi. It is the most forbidden wisdom of all. For revealing this secret in my homeland I would

165

immediately be put to death. But I know that you will not abuse that which I am prepared to entrust in you."

Pretorius had been listening to Dominique's words dumbstruck, his mouth working silently like a ruminating goat. At last he managed to form words.

"I - I have no reason to doubt you, Dominique. Neither do I doubt your knowledge of herbs and of healing. But this - this is hard to believe."

"I appreciate that, doctor, and understand your difficulty. That is why I ask to demonstrate it to you.

"The ritual can only be performed during particular alignments of the stars which occur only at certain times of the year. If we are to be ready in time for the next alignment we must make haste, for it is almost upon us. If we miss that opportunity, we will have several months to wait before conditions are right again."

"That would be too late! Last night, Frankenstein gave to understand that he was nearing success with his experiments. When exactly is this next celestial alignment?"

"I believe you refer to it as the Vernal Equinox, Doctor; two days from now, on Friday night."

* * *

"Friday night," Turhan Bey sang to himself, throwing another handful of Tana leaves to the pot, "Friday night."

He was practicing his Hammerite, and had seized upon 'Friday night' as a particularly euphonious phrase.

"Friday night, Kharis will walking," he sang to the tune of an ancient Egyptian wedding song, "Friday night, Kharis will killing."

166

Bey was in good heart. The mummy had dried out without any further damage and his preparations for the protracted rituals necessary to revive such a long dead soul were going better than he had any right to expect.

"Friday night, Doctor - " here, Bey resorted briefly to his native tongue and to a term of vulgar abuse which his limited command of Hammerite did not allow him to translate - "will screaming".

He ignored the poor scansion of the last line and launched into the chorus, dancing around the hearth and beating time with the ladle.

"And laughing I will be, until my legs is wetting, how laughing I will be."

He was about to embark upon a second verse when a furious hammering erupted within the peat cupboard. Bey danced across the room and banged on the door with his ladle in reply. This served only to antagonise the occupant, whose efforts redoubled.

Bey swore and unbolted the door. It flew open, almost catching him in the face. Inside, a young peasant woman lay full length on the floor, bound and gagged, and blackened with peat from head to toe. The moment she saw Bey she lashed out with both feet. He stepped back a pace.

"Shut your stupid bitch!" he screamed furiously, and responded with a more accurate kick of his own.

He slammed the door upon his moaning captive and shot the bolt.

"Friday night you will honour for die to Kharis' livelihood!" he jeered through the crack.

Chapter 18

Klove lay sprawled beside the laboratory trolley amidst a confusion of metal, glass, grey matter and gore. His face was buried in his hands in a futile attempt to protect himself from the Baron's frenzied attack. Frankenstein stood over him, red-faced and panting, the piece of tubing held by his side. He mopped his brow upon his sleeve.

"Weeks of preparation!" he shouted. "Two days of surgery! A perfect specimen! Ruined!"

He directed a kick at Klove's stomach. The manservant cried out and curled himself into a foetal ball. He waited for the next blow, but nothing came. There was a long silence.

When the Baron spoke again his voice was icy calm.

"Well," he said, "what's done is done. No use crying over spilt milk. Come on, up you get."

He tossed the length of hose onto the bench and reached an arm out to Klove. The young manservant whimpered and backed away until he was pressed up against the side of the trolley. The Baron chuckled, grasped him by the wrist and hauled him to his feet.

Even Frankenstein himself was surprised by the extent of the injuries he had inflicted upon Klove's face and arms. Red welts striped his cheeks. Blood was pouring from his nose and from a split in his lip. One of his eyes was closing up.

"But we must make amends for our clumsiness, mustn't we, Klove my lad?"

Frankenstein took a handkerchief from his pocket and dabbed at the blood around the manservant's mouth. Klove winced; but the pain worried him less than the Baron's sudden change of mood.

"You know why that brain was special, don't you?" he asked with the condescension of a schoolteacher addressing an idiot child. Klove nodded.

"It was fresh," he lisped through swollen lips.

"Very fresh. That's right: freshness is key to the thing," explained the Baron animatedly. "The tissues of the brain are very delicate, you see. Cut off the blood supply to the brain for too long and it is damaged beyond repair. But that last body had only been dead a few hours when you brought it to me. The accident that had been the cause of its death had not damaged the brain. When I reconnected the blood supply to it and gave it the necessary stimulant injections, it began to function again.

"It came at just the right time. My friend here," Frankenstein patted the sheeted figure on the other trolley, "cannot last forever on the slab. We can keep the blood circulating, and check the process of decay, but there are a thousand and one necessary functions controlled by the brain.

"If I am to imbue the spark of life to my creation, then he must have a brain, and he must have it soon. Do I make myself clear?"

Klove nodded, desperate to please.

"How soon?" he asked.

The Baron draped an arm around Klove's shoulder and leant in towards him conspiratorially.

"Tonight, Klove. I need a fresh brain tonight."

"I can't, master!" whined the manservant, his voice tinged with panic, "I surely would, believe me, but there ain't nobody died in the village these past two days."

Frankenstein smiled indulgently.

170

"You misunderstand me, old chap; unless you are being deliberately obtuse. You're not being obtuse, are you?"

He tightened his grip. Klove shook his head earnestly.

"I mean *really* fresh," said the Baron pointedly. "Now do you take my meaning?"

A horrified light dawned in Klove's eyes.

"No!" he exclaimed, shying away as if the Baron had threatened to hit him again, "You're asking me to do murder!"

Frankenstein shrugged.

"Am I?" he asked. "All I ask is that you find me a fresh human brain before dawn. I have not told you how you should go about procuring it.

"Neither, I might add, have I asked you to do anything that I would not do myself. Indeed, if you are unwilling or unable to make amends for your clumsiness, then I will be obliged to look about for a source close to hand. Perhaps you should not sleep too deeply tonight, lest I am tempted, eh?"

He chuckled at his own joke.

"But there again," he added disingenuously, "why choose inferior materials when such a well-bred and charming specimen lies unconscious in the guest bedroom?"

Klove was drenched with icy horror. The thought that the Baron could even consider taking a knife to the inviolable Miss Quigley appalled him beyond words. He shook his head dumbly. Frankenstein smiled, and patted him upon the shoulder.

"It would seem to be a bit of a waste, wouldn't it? Well, you just think about it while you are clearing up the mess, eh? Oh, and dispose of this - " he gestured disdainfully towards the mauled body of the carter " - while you are about it. I have no further use for it now."

"In the mean time, I shall give our sleeping beauty an injection of distilled water, in order to keep her eager protector quiet."

He walked across to the bench, opened a drawer and took out a small mahogany box. Inside was a hypodermic syringe set. He screwed the parts together, then filled the barrel from a glass beaker.

On his way out he glanced down at the grey matter which Klove was gathering into a pan.

"I wonder what he thought of that?" he mused.

* * *

For a long time after Frankenstein had gone, Klove continued to work in silence. When he had scraped as much of the mess off the floor as he could with pan and brush, he looked around for somewhere to dispose of the contents. After a moment's thought he shrugged, and emptied the pan into the carter's chest cavity. He returned the brush and pan to the broom cupboard and filled up the mop bucket.

At first, he just seemed to be moving the blood around the floor, but gradually the water in the bucket began changed colour, first to pink and then to scarlet; whilst equally slowly the flags were restored to their usual dingy grey.

Until now his actions had done nothing to betray the emotional turmoil which raged in his breast. Finally, though, something deep within him snapped. He chuckled softly.

"Old devil wants a fresh brain, does he?" he said to himself, "I'll get him one all right. Get him a good 'un, I will."

172

He picked up the bucket and emptied the contents down the nearest sink in a crimson arc.

"Thicker'n water," he muttered, snorting back his mirth. He continued to successfully contain his amusement while he rinsed out the bucket and wiped around the white porcelain sink, then returned both bucket and mop to the cupboard.

He wheeled the trolley across the room to the drop, the medieval lavatory-cum-waste disposal, which consisted of nothing more sophisticated than a hole in the floor overhanging a dizzy drop to the hillside a hundred feet below.

"Ashes to ashes, dirt to dirt, watch out below or you might get hurt," he intoned, lifting his end of the trolley. The corpse of the carter slithered off and disappeared down through the hole with scarcely a sound.

Klove spun the trolley around on its axis and shunted it into the middle of the laboratory floor, then threw back his head and let the laughter swell into a full-throated roar. He could taste the demons as they flew out of his mouth and swooped around the laboratory ceiling. Tears of joy seared his cheeks. He had found a haven in madness.

Chapter 19

Conversation in the village was still dominated by matters vampirical when Michael sat down at his accustomed seat in the Crow & Gibbet that evening. The vacuum created by the Burgomeister's lack of leadership had been filled with sullen unease.

"Somebody should do something about it!" said Goodman Brockhaus for the third time in an hour, with no more intention of doing anything about it himself than he had when he said it the first time.

"Aye, but what can we do?" whinged Bumblewicz. "We're powerless against such forces, powerless. And I've got a bad back."

In common with many of the other customers, Bumblewicz had dug out an old crucifix from his wife's jewellery box. It peeked out discreetly above the collar of his smock, hanging from a silver chain.

Others, less wealthy or not so well prepared, had pinned bulbs of garlic to their lapels. Michael was making do with a mildewed onion that he had hung around his neck on a bit of string.

"Don't sunlight kill 'em?" asked Woblinz.

"They do say so," agreed Gimmer Schwab. " 'Course, the usual way is by piercing they's hearts with good wood. Lord's dangleberries! You should see the blood spurt when you bang the bugger in. And the smell! Phaww! Worse'n you can imagine."

Michael was impressed. When it came to smells, he could imagine pretty bad ones.

"You done your own brother, din't you, Claude?" asked Tom.

Schwab inclined his head gravely.

"Bruno, my older brother by a twelve month. You remember Bruno, don't you, Bea?"

Granny Blepp nodded in her turn.

"That was back in 'forty-two, warn't it?" she asked.

"Aye, back in planting time, before we had reckoned what were goin' on. It wuz evening, and I were working late on the plot. I can still picture it, clear as yesterday.

"There I wuz, pricking out the marrer seedlings, when all of a suddenly I gets the feeling as I'm bein' watched. I turns around and who do I see standing inside the gate but Bruno - the same Bruno what I'd buried with my own hands not four days previous.

"'Klaus,' he moans like that, 'Klaus, help me. I hurts, Klaus,' he says, and he starts walking towards me with his arms stretched out like this.

"As he gets nearer I recognises the signs that he's turned into one of them, and I starts sweating and shaking and saying my prayers, what I can remember on 'em. Well, I s'pose he reckons as I've tumbled to him, 'cause all of a sudden he takes a lunge at me. I puts out my hands to protect myself just before he crashes into me and we both go down backwards onto the seedling tray with him on top.

"I'm yelling louder than a griddle full of martyrs, and struggling for all I'm worth to get him off of me. I've been heaving and tugging for nigh on a minute when I realise that he's lying on me heavy as a sack of turnips and just as still.

"I calms down a bit and finally manage to wriggle out from under him. I rolls him over and what do I see sticking out of his chest but the handle of my dibber? It's only then I realise that I wuz holding it when he attacked me, so I reckon he must've ran straight onto it and dibbered hisself to death."

176

Goodman Brockhaus shook his head and stared gloomily into his beer.

"Somebody should do something about it," he muttered.

Throughout the course of Schwab's anecdote, Bumblewicz had been glancing through the window at the gathering twilight with increasing anxiety. Finally he was able to stand it no longer. He stood up.

"Well, I think I'll be going then," he said, yawning ostentatiously, "early start tomorrow."

Ignoring an almost full flagon of ale, Goodman Brockhaus rose to his feet as well.

"Me too," he muttered sheepishly, joining Bumblewicz at the door.

"I might as well come along with you," chipped in Yeoman Woblinz, abandoning his own beer.

The exit of the three villagers signalled the start of a general exodus, and within the space of a few minutes Tom and Michael found themselves alone in each other's company.

Michael gazed around the inn, entranced by the array of half-finished and barely touched steins littering the trestle tops. He looked across at Tom, more in hope than expectation. Tom shrugged.

"Help yourself," he said, "they'll not be back tonight."

Michael felt his whole being suffused with a warm glow of anticipation. He reached for the nearest tankard.

* * *

Several hours later Tom helped Michael to his feet and led him over to the door. It was well after midnight, and when he opened the door a chilly fog blew in. Michael clung on the wall for support.

"Now, are you sure you'll be all right?" asked Tom.

"Ish bloody cold out there. Y-you cunun't give me a plaish on the floor, could you?" replied Michael, leaning towards Tom and belching beerily in his face.

"Bog off, Michael," Tom replied. "Last time I let you sleep in the bar you drank the best part of a firkin of ale and pissed in the fireplace."

With a gentle but firm shove he propelled Michael into the night and closed the door behind him.

Michael stood outside the Crow and Gibbet for a while, swaying gently in the breeze. The fog swirled around his ankles, raising gooseflesh on his legs and sending a shiver down his spine. He hiccoughed.

"Ballocksh," he muttered.

He rubbed his eyes, struggling to remember what he was meant to do next. Somewhere to sleep! That was it. With one foot planted firmly on the ground, he staggered around on his own axis like a living pair of compasses until he faced down the road.

He lurched forwards, but veering wildly to the left. The pub was coming up on him fast; just as he was bracing himself for the collision he tripped over the gimmer's bench and fell headlong to the ground. He flopped onto his back. Laughter bubbled up within him and burst out between his lips in a wet raspberry. He struggled to his feet, clutching the bench for support with one hand and the wall with the other, and waddled carefully back into the middle of the road. He tried closing one eye. That helped. He set off again.

He had only gone a few yards when a cloaked figure stepped into the road ahead of him. Michael halted in his tracks. A rush of cold sobriety doused him like a unexpected bucket of slops.

"Who be that?" He asked, fumbling for his onion. Ignoring the threat, the figure approached closer. Michael gasped.

178

"No!" he exclaimed in disbelief, "it can't be!"

The figure walked up to Michael and stopped. Moonlight illuminated his face.

"It is!" cried Michael, "it is you!"

Tears of joy welled in his eyes and spilled down his cheeks. He stumbled towards the figure and embraced him.

"But how?" he managed to interject between sobs, "I thought you were - "

" - Dead? No such luck," replied Klove, pulling Michael closer. "I've just been far away."

Enveloped in Klove's embrace, Michael was unable to see the light of insanity burning in the lad's eyes.

"Far, far away," continued Klove dreamily.

Pressing Michael's face into his cloak with one arm, Klove drew a dagger from his belt with the other and drove it to the hilt into his father's back.

Chapter 20

Constance Quigley slept on. Nothing stirred in the darkened chamber but the gentle rise and fall of her bosom. Outside, the fog had risen to the level of the window. It swirled over the surface of the glass, seeking a chink in the ancient diamond panes. It discovered a crack in the rotting casement, and an icy finger crept in.

Once inside the room, the fog took on a more substantial character. Its movements became purposeful. Like the tentacle of some blind beast it explored the windowpane until it found the wrought iron latch, then coiled around it. Slowly, the handle began to edge upwards. Metal grated faintly against metal. Finally the latch opened with a soft clunk and the window swung silently out into the night. More fog rushed in.

A hand appeared on the window ledge. A moment later, Ferdinand Frankenstein heaved himself up onto the ledge, swung his legs over the sill and dropped silently into the room. His clothes were crumpled and dirty, and his hair, wild and matted. His eyes were glazed and unfocussed. He limped heavily in the left leg.

He stumbled towards the bed.

"Good evening Ferdinand. Or should I say, Count. I suspected that you might not have the courage to appear in person."

A lamp flared. Baron Frankenstein was sitting in a chair in the corner of the room. He smiled congenially.

Ferdinand spoke. Or rather, Ferdinand's mouth worked; but the voice which emerged was not his own. It was deep and rasping, thick with evil. Frankenstein suppressed a shudder.

"Give me the girl and I will spare your life."

"Remarkable," said the Baron, quickly recovering the appearance at least of composure.

"You really must tell me how you do it. Some sort of mesmeric influence, I suppose. Sorry, old chap, but Miss Quigley stays with me."

"I have no quarrel with you."

"Nor I with you until recently. However, it seems that you have been interfering with my nephew here - "

Frankenstein indicated Ferdinand with a wave of his hand.

"This one? Take it in exchange for the girl."

"In this state? I think not. My sister would hardly thank me for returning her beloved son to her as a bloodsucking corpse.

"No, I am afraid you must learn to accept the consequences of your unruly appetites, old chap. The Ferdinand my dear Prudence was proud to call the apple of her eye is no more. Neither you nor I can restore him to his former state now.

"Perhaps it might help you to accept the loss of Miss Quigley with better grace if you think of it as compensation for the distress you have caused my family."

"You refuse to hand over the girl?"

"You have caught my meaning admirably."

"Then die!" he hissed, and Ferdinand lunged at Frankenstein.

But the Baron had anticipated his attack. He produced a large crucifix from his dressing gown and brandished it at his nephew.

Ferdinand hissed furiously and blocked out the sight of the cross with his arms. Behind his raised hands Frankenstein caught a momentary flash of the teeth of the vampire. Transferring the crucifix to his left hand he picked up a pen from the table beside him and made a note in a book.

"So it is true; you cannot abide the sight of the crucifix. How quaint."

Ferdinand turned on his heel and made for the window, but the Baron moved faster. He tossed a wreath of plaited garlic across the room. It landed upon the window catch like a quoit and hung, swinging, across the exit. Ferdinand reared back and looked around in panic for another way out.

"You will forgive me if I conduct a few experiments, I am sure. This is a unique opportunity to research the pathology of Haemophilic Porphyria, or to the vulgar, vampirism."

With affected casualness he leant across from his chair, picked up a hypodermic syringe from the table and squirted a stream of the contents at Ferdinand.

Ferdinand screamed and clutched at his face. Steam hissed from between his fingers.

"Holy water," explained the Baron, "most effective."

Ferdinand collapsed to his knees. The Baron rose out of his chair and bent over his nephew. Burying the needle of the syringe deep in the young man's shoulder, he pushed the plunger home.

No better proof of the continued operation of Ferdinand's circulatory system post mortem could be required than the speed with which the holy water coursed through his body. Within seconds the veins on his nephew's hands and face rose up and erupted into lumps. The blisters swelled and burst, and thin jets of steam blew out from the open wounds. As Frankenstein watched, his nephew's flesh began to shrivel.

Ferdinand roared out again. His spine arched in spasm and he toppled back onto the floor, his entire body shaking violently.

Frankenstein turned his nephew's face towards him in order to get a better view of his eyeballs as they swelled in their sockets.

"Fascinating," he murmured, letting Ferdinand's head fall back just before his eyeballs burst, avoiding by moments the potentially ruinous effect upon his dressing gown of the twin founts of boiling liquid which exploded into the air.

Frankenstein continued to watch with undiminished interest as his nephew's movements subsided and his roaring died away into a pathetic croak which finally dried up completely. Boiling fat ran out from the cracks that had opened in his charred skin.

When the Baron could no longer detect any sign of life in the charred corpse he gave it a nudge with his toe. With a modest ping reminiscent of clinker cooling in the grate the head snapped off and rolled away. Frankenstein consulted his pocket watch. Fifty-three seconds from the moment of injection. He turned to his notebook.

A shrill scream shattered the silence. The Baron spun around. Constance was awake and sitting up in bed. At the sight of Frankenstein she drew the sheet up to her neck.

"The master!" she cried, staring wild-eyed about the room. "He was here. I must go to him."

She began to clamber out of bed; but before she had put a foot on the floor the Baron had crossed the room, and was pressing her back into the pillow.

He had not anticipated the young woman's strength, however, nor her desperation. She twisted and writhed under his grasp, kicking and scratching like a hellcat.

184

A moment later the door flew open and Talbot burst into the room.

"Don't just stand there gawping, you bloody fool," Frankenstein shouted over his shoulder, "help me!"

Talbot sprang to the bedside. He grasped Constance's hand fervently

"Connie! Connie, my love, it's me! Lawrence - "

Constance lashed out with her free hand, gouging red stripes across Talbot's cheek.

"Hold her, damn you! She must be sedated."

Talbot clamped a beefy hand around his fiancé's other wrist, leaving the Baron free to refill his syringe from a bottle on the table. Without ceremony he hitched up Constance's nightdress, jabbed the needle into her thigh and pushed home the plunger.

The sedative took effect immediately. Constance's struggling subsided. She began to sob. Talbot tried to embrace her, but she pushed him away.

"Leave her alone!" snapped Frankenstein.

Talbot looked at the Baron curiously. He sounded proprietorial, almost jealous. Aware of the young man's suspicious glance, Frankenstein moderated his tone.

"We may be able to reason with her in due course; but for the moment she must be allowed time to herself. She must rediscover her own will."

Talbot nodded grudging assent and released his grip on Connie's wrists. As he backed away he noticed for the first time the carbonized remains on the floor.

"What in God's name is that?" he asked.

The Baron gave the charred corpse a desultory dig with his foot.

"The Count called to pay his respects. I was obliged to see him off the premises."

"The Count? Do you mean that this - "

Frankenstein scoffed.

"Of course not. Dracula would not leave the safety of his stronghold in person unless it became absolutely necessary. No, the Count's little visit was what you might term trespass by proxy."

"By proxy? I don't understand."

"No, I don't suppose you do. I have to confess that even I do not understand completely. It seems that our mutual fiend is able, not only to exert his will upon the bodies of his servants over a considerable distance, but even to project his own personality upon them. It really is quite a remarkable phenomenon."

"So who is - was - this? And what is it doing here?"

"I believe that Dracula still has an interest in your fiancé. She should be flattered. He has gone to a great deal of effort to recover her already. We must be extra vigilant from now on."

While the Baron had been speaking, Talbot had been looking down at the immolated remains on the floor. Now he bent over and picked a locket from the ashes.

"This - this was Ferdinand's!" he exclaimed. "Is this - ? It can't be!"

Frankenstein nodded neutrally.

"Yes, I am afraid so. Most tiresome."

"Tiresome! For God's sake, Baron he was your nephew! And my cherished friend! How the hell can you stand there and dismiss it as tiresome?"

Talbot wagged a finger under Frankenstein's nose.

"I tell you this much," he continued, "if I didn't think you were suffering from shock, I'd wipe that bloody sneer off your face!"

Frankenstein's day had been long and trying, and being tiraded by the oaf before him was the final straw. He slipped his hand into the pocket of his dressing gown and wrapped his fingers around the pearl handle of his revolver, secreted there as insurance in case the traditional methods of dispatching the vampire trespasser had proven less than effective. He had cocked back the hammer when there was a knock and Klove put his head around the door.

"Oh, for Christ's sake!" exploded Frankenstein, thrusting the revolver back out of sight, "what do you want?"

Klove's eyes glinted dangerously in the lamplight.

"I'm back, master" he said quietly. "I got the...meat."

Klove giggled softly at his own joke, and wiped his nose on his sleeve.

"Meat? What the hell are you - oh, I see."

Frankenstein turned back to Talbot.

"I must go now. I have work to do - important work. You will stay here and guard Miss Quigley. Do not attempt to engage her in conversation; do not let her rise, and under no circumstances must you leave the room, not even for a moment. Do I make myself clear?"

"Yes, but what if - ?"

" - I am reasonably sure that Dracula will make no further attempt to abduct her tonight; but if anything untoward does occur, just pull the bell-rope. We will not be far away. I can be here in seconds.

"The sedative I have administered is a strong one. Do not worry if Miss Quigley falls asleep again. Let her rest. Now that the hypnotic spell is broken, it can do her nothing but good."

Before Talbot could protest the Baron swept out of the room, closing the door behind him.

* * *

Down in the cellar laboratory Klove had already lit the lamps and laid out the Baron's surgical equipment. On the trolley in place of the much-abused body of the carter was a burlap sack, dripping blood. Frankenstein followed Klove down the stairs.

Something in his manservant's manner was making the Baron distinctly uneasy. Every now and then Klove would snigger to himself, as if he had just recollected a private joke. It was rare enough in itself to hear the young man giving vent to any expression of amusement; but this was no ordinary laughter. There was humour in it, certainly, but also something chilling, even threatening. Although Klove's behaviour was annoying Frankenstein, he found himself putting an uncharacteristic curb on his tongue.

Another aspect of Klove's behaviour that was giving the Baron cause for concern was the lad's seeming lack of interest in his 'medication'. By Frankenstein's reckoning, Klove had now been without morphine for something in the order of twenty-four hours. Normally this would have been enough to reduce him to quivering desperation; yet here he was, laughing to himself and displaying every sign of contentment. Could Klove have found his own supply of the drug? The Baron dismissed the thought as unlikely, but was unable to come up with any other explanation.

Klove walked over to the trolley ahead of Frankenstein and untied the cord that bound the neck of the sack. Michael's head lolled out of the bag, his face daubed with his own blood and his eyes staring blankly, frozen in his final moment of dumb bewilderment.

While Klove struggled to pull the sack down and out from under the corpse, Frankenstein inspected Michael's head, turning it this way and that. He reached

188

over to the array of surgical implements and selected a pair of gleaming steel callipers, then opened the legs of the instrument and closed them gently on either temple.

He prised the callipers off Michael's head and measured the gap against a ruler.

"Poor cranial development, very poor. Verging on the moronic, I would say," he muttered, making a note in his book.

"So what do we know about this fine fellow?" he asked over his shoulder.

Klove sniggered.

"Who's to tell, master?" he replied, "some mother's son, some poor bugger's father".

"That I doubt," said the Baron without looking up, "I can't believe that any woman would willingly share her bed with a foul specimen like this for love nor money."

"Maybe not for love, Master..." replied Klove.

The Baron left off measuring for a moment and looked curiously at Klove. The lad's flippant, even garrulous tone troubled him. And was it his imagination, or was there a hint of a sneer in the young manservant's voice each time he addressed the Baron as 'Master'? After a few moment's uncomfortable contemplation, during which Klove continued to return his gaze unwaveringly, with an air of faint amusement, Frankenstein shrugged off his musings and returned to his work. After all, he reasoned, the lad had been through a lot recently. And, of course, he had just committed murder.

"You've done well, Klove my boy. Perhaps we should give you some medication now, as a little reward? Not so much that you are unable to work the pump during the operation, you understand, but something to help you relax. What do you say to that?"

Klove shook his head.

"I've not felt so relaxed like what I am now for a good long while, Master, thanking you kindly an' all. Maybe a bit later, eh, when we're done? I been looking forward to watching this."

Frankenstein shrugged.

"Very well," he replied. "Bring the pump closer and pass me the hollow needles. We must restart the circulation of the blood without delay."

Within moments the Baron had fallen silent, immersed in his work. Occasionally he would mutter a single word of command to Klove, but in truth even that was unnecessary. Klove had assisted him in similar operations so many times that he knew his role perfectly.

As soon as Frankenstein had inserted the needles into the corpse's veins and arteries, Klove started to turn the handle of the pump. Blood began to move sluggishly along the clear glass tube into the aerator and back into the body. He positioned himself so that he was able to turn the handle with one hand and pass the Baron the tools and equipment he needed with the other.

Frankenstein placed a circular clamp over Michael's forehead and tightened the screws. Klove chuckled. His late father looked as if he was sporting a gleaming steel halo. The Baron paused for a moment, looking pensive.

"Cranial saw," he said at last.

Klove handed him a gleaming, ivory-handled saw. The Baron positioned it carefully on Michael's forehead.

"Now we cut," he said.

190

Chapter 21

"Cut!" shouted Fisher.

Peter Cushing shielded his eyes, and peered beyond the studio lights at the silhouetted figure of the director.

"Was that all right, Terry?" he asked. "I nearly fluffed the 'cranial saw' line. I forgot the name of the dashed thing for a moment."

"It worked rather well; made you look pensive," replied Fisher. "I thought you were acting."

"Heaven forefend!" exclaimed Cushing with a smile.

"We'll break for lunch now and meet back at -" Fisher consulted his watch "- half-past three for the head sawing."

"It can be earlier if you want," Cushing replied, delicately expressing the collective concerns of the cast and studio team around him, "we could all just grab a sandwich and be back in an hour?"

If Fisher recognised the intent behind Cushing's suggestion, he didn't show it.

"No," he said blithely, "we all deserved a break. Half-three it is. Continuity," he continued, "Take a sketch of Mick's wounds and transfer them to the FX head."

The effects junior stepped into the pool of lights with a sketch pad and pencil. There was a little less spring in his step. This was the second day in a row he would have to work right through his lunch break in order to get the work done in time for the return of the rest of the crew.

Peter Cushing gave a sudden exclamation and lifted the saw from Ripper's forehead.

"My dear boy," he said, rubbing gently at the light indentations that the teeth of the saw had left in his skin, "I'm so sorry. I quite had forgotten that you were still in the realm of the living."

Ripper continued to lie on the trolley, silent and unmoving, with his eyes shut.

"Mick?"

Cushing shook his fellow actor gently by the shoulder. Ripper emitted an unintelligible grunt and rolled onto his side. Cushing smiled at Troughton.

"Would you believe it, Pat? He's fallen asleep."

Cushing put his mouth to the actor's ear.

"Michael!" he murmured gently, "Scene's over."

He shook Ripper again and the actor awoke with an exclamation.

"Wha - ? What you doin', Klovey boy?"

He rubbed his eyes and looked around.

"Peter!" he exclaimed. "Just resting my eyes. Are we ready to shoot yet?"

Cushing chuckled.

"All done and dusted, old boy. You played your part with Strasbergian conviction."

Ripper was still groggy, but managed a derisive grunt.

Cushing offered Ripper his hand and helped him sit up on the trolley.

Ripper swivelled and let his legs hang over the side. He waited obediently, still a little disoriented from his doze, while the junior made an approximate sketch of quantity and disposition of the Kensington Gore daubed on his cheeks and forehead.

While he worked, Cushing continued to chat with his old friend.

"You know that you woke up in character, don't you Mike?" he asked. Ripper nodded ruefully.

"I'm not surprised. Recently I've been having recurring dreams in which I'm a real peasant in a real village – well, a Hammer village, if you know what I mean - and all sorts of horrific events are taking place around me."

The effects junior closed his pad and thanked Ripper. Ripper stood up and stretched. Cushing draped his cardigan over his shoulders, Ripper picked up his script and the two strolled across the lot together.

"You've had roles in so many Hammer films, I'm not surprised that you end up acting in your sleep," said Cushing, "Sometimes the films all seem to merge into one. I'm not complaining, not in the least. I have a great deal to thank the company for. But the scripts! My goodness! Sometimes I despair."

"At least they give you a range of roles and characters," Ripper replied. "I get the same ruddy part whatever I'm in! I'm sure they've only got the one character sheet for me. 'Doomed derelict', he's called, and the description goes something like 'Michael establishes his character by committing an uncouth act or minor felony. He visits the pub' - "

" – 'Inn'," corrected Cushing.

"'Inn', you're right. 'He visits the inn, gets drunk, staggers out and into the clutches of - delete as appropriate - vampire, werewolf, mummy, etcetera'."

Cushing chuckled.

"It's your own fault," he said. "You're just too good at dying. I've never heard a death rattle to touch yours, I give you my word. Anyway, swings and roundabouts, old chap; don't I recall you having a romp in a cellar with several of Christopher's voluptuous brides last week?"

"A romp? Hardly. Just another messy death. One of the Brides got a bit carried away and actually grazed my neck. Do you suppose that makes me a vampire?"

* * *

They had reached the canteen. Cushing opened the door and stood aside to let the women from the typing pool emerge before they entered. They picked up trays and joined the queue at the counter.

"So if you could persuade the scriptwriters to give you another role for once, what part would you want?" asked Cushing, ladling soup from a tureen into a bowl and helping himself to a bread roll.

"That's a good question. I'll have to think about that for a minute," replied Ripper. He inspected a few cellophane-wrapped sandwiches before settling for the Coronation Chicken.

It was not until both had sat down at the same table as Patrick Troughton and started their meals that he spoke again.

"I'll tell you what I'd have them write for me, Peter; a comic sleuth. That would suit me down to the ground. You know, deerstalker, cape, pipe, the lot; but he'd be a bit of a bumbler and would only uncover the bad guy by happy accident."

"They'd still want you to die at the end," said Troughton through a mouthful of sandwich.

"That's exactly what I've been telling him," said Cushing, waving his spoon in emphasis. "He's a victim of his own success; he's just too good at dying."

Ripper gave a mirthless laugh and took a sip of tea.

"I've been having a good old moan to Peter about the parts they give me," he explained. "Sometimes I feel as if I'm playing the same character in every film."

"I have a theory about exactly this point," said Troughton, fixing both of them with glittering eyes. "It's long been my suspicion that all of Hammer's horror films are just incidents taken from the history of a single village.

194

"It's a small hamlet, deep in the Carpathians, I think, with a touch of Zummerzet about the accent. Nineteenth century, by-and-large, with occasional forays into the eighteenth when the budget will stretch, and lapses into the present when times is hard. We'll call it Karnstein, for the sake of argument.

"It's a quiet backwater, populated with simple, hard working folk who expect nothing more at the end of the day but a pint and a handful of barmaid down the pub - "

" - Inn," corrected Ripper and Cushing simultaneously.

" - Inn," Troughton conceded. "But what the poor sods actually get is an endless succession of blood-curdling monsters rampaging around the countryside, cutting a swathe through the peasantry and absconding with the flower of their womanhood."

"It's an interesting notion," said Cushing, wiping the corner of his mouth with his napkin, "Do you suppose that there are times between films when nothing much happens? Do the poor citizens of Karnstein get weekends and bank holidays off?"

"I don't think so. I reckon that you can lay the films end to end and construct one seamless narrative. It's a sort of Gothic soap opera. Unfortunately, Karnstein happens to be a very busy place; a supernatural Clapham Junction, where all manner of horrors meet."

"And are your Karnstinians oblivious to the fact that their lives are anything out of the ordinary?" asked Ripper.

"Absolutely," Troughton replied, "They know no other way. They assume that life would be similar wherever they lived. Perhaps it would. Maybe they are a chosen people. Most of the time they're fairly stoical about it, but every now and then they decide that they have had enough, arm themselves with flaming brands and pitchforks and march on one or other of the castles."

"- and through this endless nightmare, Mike's alter ego stumbles drunkenly from death to gory death," said Cushing. "I like it."

"So how come I never learn from my demises?" asked Ripper. "Is my character so thick that it never occurs to him not to leave the p- inn of an evening?"

Troughton thought for a moment.

"Well, you have to admit that based on his form to date, he doesn't seem to be overburdened with brains," Troughton winked impishly at Cuushing.

"Thanks a bunch, Pat!" said Ripper with feeling.

"But maybe it's more the case that you simply don't *remember* your deaths," Troughton continued, "Perhaps your memory is wiped clean every time you are reincarnated. It would create all sorts of problems and paradoxes if your character became aware that he was effectively immortal."

"And am I - is he - immortal? Is there no way that he can escape his cycle of violent death and hungover reincarnation? You've got to give me a break here, Pat, or I'm never going to play my comedy Holmes."

"I'm not sure about that, Mike," replied Troughton, solemnly shaking his head. "I mean, whatever spiteful deity presides over this savage little universe has to have his bit of fun."

"It's the title of the Father Brown story in reverse," observed Cushing; "not the Hammer of God, but the God of Hammer,"

"Very good, Peter," said Troughton appreciatively. "Carreras, father, son and holy bloody ghost."

A tableful of the film crew rose as one and headed for the door.

"Come on Pat: back to the fray," said Cushing.

Troughton pushed back his chair and stood up.

"Maybe your character has to earn his escape from the cycle of rebirth like the Buddhists, Mike. Perhaps he has to redeem himself through some sort of selfless act. Or there again, maybe not."

Ripper, who was not needed on set for the rest of the day, continued to sit at the table after the other two actors had gone, finishing his tea and thinking. The idea of Troughton's consistent Hammer world appealed to him. Many times over his acting career, the feeling had come over him as he walked onto the set that he was not assuming a role, but stepping into the shoes of a character who already existed in his own right. Furthermore, he knew that this was not an eccentricity peculiar to him alone; many of his fellow professionals - sensible, no-nonsense types, not the Lee Strasberg trendies - had made similar observations.

Christopher Lee, the company philosopher, was fond of quoting a Chinese proverb that was remarkably apposite. How did it go? Ripper struggled without success to recall it, and was still racking his brains when someone tapped him on the shoulder. He looked up. It was Tom Hereward, the assistant sound editor.

"Blimey, Mick I've called your name three times," he said.

"Sorry Tom. I was lost in metaphysical speculation."

"They can't touch you for it. Is now a good time to borrow you for that bit of dubbing?" he asked.

Ripper looked at his watch.

"Go on, then," he replied, "It's not going to take long, is it?"

"It shouldn't do; we've got everything set up ready."

* * *

The editing suite was a rather grand title for the maze of tiny interconnecting rooms to which it referred. One of the several elegantly proportioned drawing rooms of Oakley Court had been subdivided with partition walls, and over the years several doors had been knocked through existing walls into the overbutler's quarters. Everywhere there were cables; covering the floor in a confused and hazardous tangle, and trailing overhead, looped over wooden struts.

The only area which was even half tidy was the projection room, and it was into that slightly more comfortable space that Hereward ushered Ripper.

At one end of the room were a grubby projection screen and a pair of elderly speaker cabinets. Several square hatches had been cut in the wall opposite, through which peered a row of curious film projectors. Along one wall were stacked the chairs that would be set out in rows at the end of every week for the viewing of the rushes. Because of the lack of space, the projection room also served as a second dubbing studio.

A table and chair had been positioned in the middle of the room. On it stood a heavy microphone, easily fifteen years old, and to its left, an equally antiquated set of headphones. On the other side stood a reading lamp and a tumbler of water. Ripper sat down in the chair and arranged his dog-eared script on the table next to the glass. Tom helped him on with the headphones and left the room, closing the door behind him.

A few moments later his voice came through on the headphones.

"Could you give me a sound-check, please Mick?"

Ripper edged his chair forward.

"Testing, testing, one, two, three...the pork in Patagonia is putrid, but the sausages in San Salvador are superb."

"A bit more…"

Ripper rummaged in the shoe-box of his memory for something else to say.

"Well, now that we have seen each other," he said, "if you'll believe in me, I'll believe in you."

"That's fine. My goodness, we are dwelling on the higher plane today, aren't we? Down to earth with a bump, I fear. Are you ready to record?"

Ripper pulled his script into the light of the reading lamp.

"Go ahead," he replied.

The overhead lights dimmed. A moment later a flickering white rectangle lit the projection screen.

A hand appeared in close-up, filling the screen. It dangled, unmoving, over the edge of a table or bed. The skin was waxy and pallid; the fingertips, blackened. A ragged wound ran right around the wrist, held together by clumsy sutures.

One of the fingers twitched. Ripper leant towards the microphone.

Chapter 22

Michael groaned. He had woken up with some hangovers in his time, but this one had to take the cake. At the thought of cake, a wave of nausea swept through him. He swallowed hard and opened his eyes. The room revolved with stately grandeur.

He struggled to sit upright. Oh ballocks, he thought, I can't move. It's the booze; it's finally done for me like what the Father always said it would. He tried wiggling his fingers. At least they seemed to be working. With a superhuman effort he craned his neck and peered down at his hands.

They seemed further away than usual. More than that, they had taken on a sickly greenish cast in the night. Most disturbing of all, however, was the fact that he was tied to a trolley.

On the off-chance that it might all be a bad dream he closed his eyes and banged his head on the trolley. Fireworks exploded upon the inner surface of his eyelids. He opened his eyes again. No: this was as good as things were going to get. Leather bands still crossed his chest and legs, and bound his wrists to his sides. He had a sudden urge to pass water.

Taking a deep breath, he strained against the chest restraint. Needles of pain tattooed across his midriff. Abandoning that particular avenue of exploration before he ruptured himself, he tried wrenching the wristbands. After a few seconds of grunting exertion he felt something give. He looked down at his right wrist. Blood was welling up from a popped suture and gathering in the scar around his wrist. He discontinued his efforts. No point in getting his arm free, he reasoned, if he had to pull his own hand off to do so.

Michael's head was throbbing. He felt sick, he was dying for a piss and something awful had happened to his hand in the night. Person or persons unknown had tied him to a bed, for what unspeakable purpose he did not care to speculate. He had had enough.

With a muted snarl he twisted within his bonds, forcing his right shoulder up off the padded surface of the trolley. The trolley rocked; both of the right hand wheels lifted off the ground for a moment, then dropped back with a jarring jolt. But the action seemed to have had some effect: Michael thought that he detected a slackening in the tension of the band across his chest. He repeated the exercise with his other shoulder.

The trolley rocked violently to the left, found a point of unstable equilibrium on two wheels, teetered, then overbalanced and crashed to the floor, pinning him face-down.

* * *

Victor, the eighth Baron Frankenstein, lay on top of his bed, fully clothed but for one shoe, which lay on the floor nearby. One of the panes of the chamber window rattled in sympathy with his snores.

He had kept going through the long hours of the operation with a combination of stimulant drugs and sheer willpower. As soon as he had tied off the last suture, the accumulated exhaustion had hit him like a physical blow. It had taken all his remaining strength to get as far as his bed before passing out.

A gentle tap on the door did not awaken him. He was not aware of the slow turning of the handle, nor did he hear the creak of the door.

"Master!"

Klove's stuck his head round the door. He watched Frankenstein for a moment or two, then withdrew, content that the Baron would sleep for a good while yet.

As he approached Miss Constance's door, he decided to permit himself a moment of harmless idolatry. When he tried the handle, however, he found himself shut out. He bent down and peered through the keyhole.

She was still asleep, as was her fiancé, slumped in an armchair beside her bed. Klove craned his neck and peered down at the floor. Before falling asleep, Talbot had wedged a chair under the doorknob. Klove nodded in approval.

Klove felt no jealousy towards Talbot, even though the young man held Miss Constance's heart and would eventually have her hand. As the one whom Miss Constance herself had chosen to be her lover and protector, he was touched by her grace, and to be respected.

The Baron, however, had no more right than Klove himself to entertain thoughts about Miss Constance, especially the sort of thoughts he was entertaining. Klove was prepared to do whatever was necessary to protect her from his lascivious attentions.

Like all the other occupants of the Castle, Klove, too, should have been asleep in his bed. He had been awake now for over forty-eight hours, and the only thing keeping him going was the anticipation of seeing his insane revenge completed. He rubbed his hands together, cackled madly and headed down the stairs towards the laboratory.

* * *

Michael was still lying face-down on the flags with the trolley on top of him when Klove entered. Klove's heart sank. What a tragedy it would be for some stupid accident to rob him of his revenge! Taking the stairs two at a time, he was beside the trolley in moments, grunting with the effort of standing it back up again.

He gave Michael a cursory once over. He was bleeding here and there, and his nose was a bit squashed, but there didn't seem to be any major damage. He was conscious, and to judge by the language he was using, his brain - such as it was - seemed to be working as normal.

Klove leant over Michael and peered into his eyes as he had seen Frankenstein do to the victims of his earlier experiments. He did not really know what he was looking for, but he supposed that it would be obvious enough if anything was wrong.

As Klove's face came into focus Michael's torrent of invective faltered, and dried up. He gasped.

"No!" he exclaimed in disbelief. "It can't be!"

Klove realised with intense irritation that Michael had not the slightest recollection of their reunion the night before. It had taken every ounce of his resolve to take his father's life: the least the old bastard could do was remember it.

"It is!" cried Michael. "It is you!"

Tears of joy welled in his eyes and spilled down his cheeks. He struggled with his restraints again, frustrated at not being able to embrace his lost son.

"But how, Klovey boy?" he managed to interject between sobs, "I - "

" - Thought I was dead? Well, you was wrong, wasn't you?"   He reached across Michael's chest and started unbuckling the straps. "Not that I wouldn't as happy dead as alive oftentimes."

He sat Michael up on the trolley. Michael felt the room swim.

"'Tain't easy being the son of a whore," said Klove bitterly. "Difficult to hold your head up in public, when the only home you've ever known is a brothel.

"Not as I held Momma's trade against her; she had to make a living, whatever way she could. She tried her best to give me a decent start; and the other women too. They showed me how I could still have my self-respect; at least when I was at home."

Michael felt too ill to concentrate on his son's speech for long. He looked around for a receptacle, just in case he had need of it.

"PAY ME BLOODY HEED!" roared Klove, grasping Michael by the chin and wrenching the old man's head back to face his own.

Michael whimpered. All the uncertainties of his current situation seemed to be congealing into something frightening and dangerous.

"Don't be angry with me, Klovey boy," he whined. "I feels sick; can't seem to think straight."

Klove dug his fingernails into Michael's cheeks.

"You will bloody listen! You'll listen till I'm done!"

Michael nodded sheepishly.

"Good. Where was I?

"'Tis a good spur, living in the gutter; knowing there's no way out but up. Or so I thought. I had a brain, and I wuzz willing enough to work hard, God knows. Why, I were even sweet on a girl; in time, I hoped to tell her how I felt t'wards her.

"But on the eve of my manhood, momma told me the truth about myself: and that's one thing I can never forgive her for."

Tears welled in Klove's eyes and spilled down his cheeks.

"Can you imagine how it feels to be told that your natural father is the most useless, disgusting, evil-smelling old twat what ever soiled God's clean earth? That your grandfather wuzz a bottle and your grandmother a midden? Eh? Can you, father?"

Klove's face was within inches of Michael's now. Michael felt himself trembling.

"I didn't believe her at first; I'd never seen you in the Lair. I've thrown better'r'n you out on their arses. My God, I know she couldn't afford to be fussy, but how could she?

"I never could work out how you scraped the money together. Did you pick somebody's pocket? Eh? How much did I cost? Was I a five groat quickie?"

Klove buried his head in his hands and sobbed uncontrollably. Michael's heart went out to him.

"I-I always fancied Elsie," he faltered; then stopped mid-phrase. He ran his tongue around the inside of his mouth and over his lips. Something - everything - felt wrong. His cheeks felt rubbery; his palate too high; he seemed to have more teeth than he was accustomed to. But everything was too strange at the moment to pay much attention to minor alterations to his anatomy.

"She were a handsome woman, even when she wuzz a lass," he continued. "I were always tryin' get me hands up her skirts, but she never looked at me twice. No woman ever has.

"I only gone with her the once. Back end of the 'fifties, it would have been. You'd be too young to remember the Brethren, wouldn't you? They banned the booze outright: ale, wine, brandy, the lot. Didn't know what to do with meself. Ended up with a bit of money spare and spent it on her." He paused again, chewing at the inside of his mouth, then chuckled.

206

"She threw me out first time. Telled me not to bother to come back lessen I washed head to toe an' all points between. Had to borrow new breeches an' hose an' all. Even then she didn't want to see my face. Made me do it - "

"SHUT UP!" screamed Klove, clutching Michael by the throat and trying to choke him into silence, "do you think I want to know the bloody details?"

Michael shut up, even though he had thought exactly that.

"I could have had 'most any man in the village for a father," spat Klove. "The Burgomeister, with his wealth and position; the Doctor for his learning. God knows, I wouldn't have even minded being John the Smith's son. Leastwise he makes an honest living. But no, it had to be you... You what turned me into a monster."

Klove grasped Michael by the wrist and pulled him to its feet. Michael swayed precariously. He seemed to be looking down on everything from a height considerably greater than was usual or proper. Klove let go of his arm and Michael clung to the side of the trolley for support.

Klove dashed across the room to a sheeted article of furniture and dragged it towards the trolley. Brass castors rattled across the flags. Klove had started giggling again through his tears. As he came to a halt in front of his father, a deep throated, demonic laugh burst from him like a clap of thunder.

"Look, father!" he shrieked, stripping off the dustsheet in one sweeping movement to reveal a full-length cheval mirror.

Michael stared. The creature in the mirror stared back.

It was a parody of a man; an ungodly joke at the expense of human dignity.

It was tall, standing a good twelve inches above the madman beside it, even barefoot and stark naked. Its body was crazed with a network of puckered, weeping wounds, sewn up with rough stitches. A ragged seam from thorax to groin was held together with bright metal staples. Its legs were dark, hairy and muscular. The trunk, by contrast, was pallid, frail and pigeon-chested, while the slender arms might have belonged to a woman or youth. The whole body was covered in bruises, and the extremities - its fingertips and toes, ears and eyelids - were withered and blackened.

The face was battered almost beyond recognition. Almost, but not quite: underneath the swelling and the clumsy needlework Michael still recognised the features of Bartolmas Mullerson. Yet that was not possible: Bartolmas had been crushed to death under a cartload of pumpkins this Harvest just gone, and Michael had seen him into his grave. Almost followed him into it, in fact, but that was another story.

"Can't be," he muttered, raising his hands to his face. The creature did the same.

"No!"

Michael's shriek rang through the laboratory like a cracked bugle. He stumbled backwards, desperate to deny the horror before him, yet unable to tear his eyes from the image in the glass. He crashed into the trolley, sending it spinning across the room. The sound of Klove's laughter rose above his screams. He covered his ears.

The edge of the worktop dug into the back of his thighs. He began to edge along the wall. A small recess opened up behind him unexpectedly and he stumbled back into it. Suddenly the floor disappeared from under him and he dropped out of sight with a yelp.

Klove's gleeful grin hit the flags with a thud.

"Nooo!" he screamed in horror, leaping across the room.

208

Michael was clinging to the lip of the Drop by his fingertips. A chilly morning breeze cooled his ankles. He heard with remarkable clarity the staccato clack of a dislodged fragment of masonry, as it bounced down the mountainside far below.

Klove dropped to his knees and stared down at his father. The creature looked back up at him beseechingly.

"Help me Klovey boy!" he pleaded.

Klove's face clouded over with a confusion of contradictory emotions. Michael's fingertips started to slip on the greasy stone.

"Please, son!"

Michael lost his grip.

Klove's hand shot out and grasped Michael's wrist. Muscle quivered. Sinews snapped. Sweat beaded on Klove's brow. Grunting with exertion he started to haul the creature back through the shaft. Then, instantaneously, all resistance vanished. Klove was flung violently backwards, cracking his head on the flags.

He sat up and looked down at his right hand. He was still holding the creature's hand firmly by the wrist. Blood dripped from the bloody stump. A finger twitched spasmodically.

A shriek rang out from the Drop and trailed away to silence.

Chapter 23

In the woods behind the Abbey, Dominique hummed to herself as she gathered Tana leaves. The tune was that of a lullaby her mother had sung to her as a child. She had long since forgotten the words, but the tune comforted her still.

Ever since she had offered to perform the zombi ritual for Pretorius, she had been ill at ease. That was reasonable enough: Ju-ju was forbidden knowledge, and in sharing its secrets with the Doctor she was committing an uncountenanceable offence. But here in the gloom of the woods something else was disturbing her, something she could not put her finger on.

As she bent down to start on the next bush, the disquiet that had been nagging at the back of her mind suddenly came into focus. Somebody had been here before her. On this shrub as on the last, the top few leaves had been stripped from the stems. A shiver trickled down her back.

Who else could have been gathering Tana leaves? Contact with the Tana plant was taboo. None but the chosen could touch it, and then only after elaborate purification rituals. It was inconceivable, surely, that another Ju-ju priest could be residing in the valley unbeknownst to her.

She was aware that the old wisdom was not the exclusive preserve of the African peoples, but she found no comfort in that; Tana magic was potent and unpredictable, like a wild animal. Few could control it; in the hands of any but the most experienced it would bring only disaster.

Further on she found more evidence that she was not the first visitor to the woods this morning. On the ground beside the bushes she came upon the impression of a footprint in the soft leaf mould. It was recent, perhaps less than an hour old. She felt the hair rise on the nape of her neck.

She picked the last few leaves as quickly as she could, glancing over her shoulder at every sound. As soon as she had gathered enough she pinned up her apron and hurried out of the wood.

* * *

With a shudder of relief Turhan Bey shut the door of the peat cutter's cottage behind him, threw the pouch of Tana leaves onto the table and hurried across to the hearth. Squatting down on his haunches he warmed his icy hands over the smouldering peat. All being well, he though, that should be the last time he would have to quit the warmth of the cottage until tonight. After that he would be able to leave this vile, damp sewer of a place behind him forever and return to the warmth and civilisation of his native land.

The bitch in the cupboard started her infernal pounding on the door again. Bey muttered darkly, and rose to his feet. If it hadn't been absolutely necessary to keep her alive for the ritual he would have cut her throat some time ago. He consoled himself with the thought that she had only a few hours left in which to irritate anybody.

The remains of several simple meals lay scattered over the tabletop. Bey picked up a stale piece of bread and headed for the bedroom. As he passed the peat cupboard he rapped on the cupboard door, and chuckled evilly at the frenzied response.

The temple was complete. The mummy of Kharis lay in state on the bed-turned-altar, with the sacrificial knife by its side. The Tana potion had turned an alarming bilious green. He picked up an elaborate ritual spoon and stirred in a few fresh leaves. The mixture was almost ready.

On a table beside the bed stood a tiny phial of black glass. Bey pulled out the stopper and sprinkled a few drops of the contents onto the crust. Whilst he would have relished her struggle and the sound of her screams as the knife came down, reluctantly, he knew that such perverse pleasures did not stand up against the risk of something going wrong. Drugged, she would put up no resistance and could cause no trouble.

He tiptoed back through to the other room and stood outside the cupboard door. The girl had stopped kicking, and all Bey could hear was the faint sound of her sobbing in the dark. He drew back the bolt and opened the door. She lay supine, looking up at him through hollow, red-rimmed eyes. She had not eaten for a couple of days, or slept either, by the look of her. He leant over her and pulled the gag down to her neck.

"Hungry?" he asked, and thrust the bread into her mouth. She ate ravenously. As soon as she had swallowed he pulled the gag back over her mouth and shut the door upon her again.

* * *

As Dominique neared the abbey, she saw Joachim straighten up from his work and cast a moody eye at the clouds gathering overhead. She called his name across the graveyard. He gave her a cursory nod and returned to his digging.

Dominique was well aware that Joachim was not happy about the business of the night ahead: but as she had explained to him, this was the last task they would ever have to perform in service. Tomorrow they would wake as free people, under obligation to no-one. From that day on they would sleep when they chose and rise when they wanted.

More than two years had elapsed since they had fled Haiti; their names and the offences they had committed had long been forgotten. Armed with the papers that Pretorius had draughted for them, they would be able to complete the last leg of their journey without attracting undue attention. Dominique had salted away enough money to buy themselves a smallholding or business when they were safely back in their native land.

As Dominique drew close, she heard the hollow clunk of Joachim's spade striking hollow wood. She peered down into the hole. Joachim flung out a last load of earth, then abandoned his spade and brushed the rest of the dirt off the coffin lid with his hands.

"Well done, my love," said Dominique. "Let me help."

Joachim grunted non-committally and pointed to a coil of rope on the grass. Dominique threw it down to him. A minute later he emerged, bringing one end of the rope with him. Bracing himself at one end of the hole he drew in the slack and pulled on the rope.

Dominique stood beside him, enjoying the swell of his biceps and the landscape of his back as he heaved the coffin inch by laborious inch out of the hole. As soon as it was within reach, she leant over and helped him drag it across and onto the grass.

The coffin had been interred for many years, and the wood of which it was constructed was cracked and rotten. Joachim prised the lid off with the edge of his spade and flung it aside.

"Good," murmured Dominique. She had wanted to leave no room for doubt in the doctor's mind about the efficacy of the ritual; no accusations of fakery, of having simply woken some poor peasant from a drug-induced catatonia. No, she thought to herself, there would be no uncertainty with this corpse.

Joachim plucked up the courage to look down the open coffin. He shuddered.

It was little more than a skeleton, dressed in the severe black garb of the Brethren. Strips of mummified grey flesh were stretched tight over its skull and hands. Here and there, bones showed through tears in its mildewy skin. Empty

214

eye sockets stared back at him accusingly. A worm emerged from the septum of its nose and explored the novel sensation of fresh air. Joachim turned away from the ghastly sight. Dominique laid a hand on his arm.

"Be brave, my love," she murmured. "Keep your courage. Your part is almost done."

She touched his cheek, turning his head towards her, and fixed him with her gaze. Her eyes flashed and sparkled from deep within, like black opals. Joachim felt her spirit flooding into him, making him strong again. He smiled at her and made sounds that were unintelligible to all but her.

"I love you, too," she replied.

Joachim knelt down and scooped up the skeleton. As he rose, he felt it crack at the base of the spine. The bottom half of the body, weighed down by heavy leather boots, tumbled back into the coffin. Joachim made to pick it up.

"No matter," said Dominique, "the top half is enough. Come: lay it down here."

Joachim placed the torso on the raised stone slab of a nearby tomb. He stood back, swatting at the flecks of grave mould which clung to his chest and forearms.

"Good. Now, stay here while I go and get the doctor."

Dominique started towards the Abbey house, then stopped in her tracks and turned back to Joachim.

"Just a few more hours," she said, her eyes aglow with excitement and apprehension, "and we will be free forever!"

Chapter 24

Perhaps the god who watches over the Vale of Walach prefers to manage his diocese through the medium of coincidence. It has its advantages. Outright miracles can cause talk, even in an environment as accustomed to supernatural phenomena as Karnstein. Coincidence, even when stretched paper-thin, can still provide cover against the aspirations of any curious soul who might be seeking an easy route to faith through the direct observation of divine intervention at work.

Of course, it may be simply that the gods are perverse. Hard to tell really, gods being the enigmatic creatures they are.

Whatever the case, the only witness to events about to take place on the mountainside below Castle Frankenstein was a goat, which was making a late breakfast of the mean shrubbery that clung to the rocky slopes. As it shambled between bushes it paused for a moment and regarded the mutilated corpses of the Carter and Michael suspiciously.

The bodies lay where they had finally come to rest after their disposals through the drop and their consequent tumbles down the mountainside, separated by only a matter of hours. The Carter's corpse was folded double over a boulder: while nearby, Michael's lay flat on its back with the skull cap hanging open on its fleshy hinge. The goat sniffed curiously at the skull cavity.

Then it pricked up its ears. It heard something; a continuous wailing note, faint and far off, but growing louder by the second. It straightened up and looked around nervously. The noise swelled to a deafening shriek that was instantly cut short as Frankenstein's monstrous creation plummeted out of the sky and crashed onto the rocks a few feet away.

Blood spurted out of the stump of the creature's wrists like chianti out of a wine-skin, spraying the animal's flanks. It bolted down the hillside, bleating in distress.

It missed the best bit. The monster's head smashed into the ground with such force that the recently stapled skullcap burst its fixings, shot clean off and flew through the air, landing with a clatter on the rocks further downhill.

For a few moments nothing happened. Then a small ball of grey matter - a very small ball - slithered out of the creature's skull cavity and dropped gently onto the ground.

It began to roll slowly down the hill, like a whole egg-yolk, slithering down the side of a mixing bowl, picking up dust, twigs and gravel as it went. Propelled by the agency of gravity alone it meandered around a boulder, disappeared under a shrubby bush and emerged the other side, rolled along an inclined stone slab and slid gently over the edge to plop neatly into Michael's cranium. The slight change in weight caused Michael's head to turn to one side, flipping his skull cap shut. With a faint zipping sound the ragged wound around his head healed up, leaving only a scar lost amongst the many wrinkles that furrowed his brow.

A few moments later Michael groaned and sat up, clutching his head in his hands.

Another day, another hangover, he thought; another blind panic, trying to work out where the hell he was. It was always the same. He couldn't help wishing that just once, something out of the ordinary would happen to him.

* * *

Talbot sat bolt upright in his chair, suddenly wide awake and aware that something had wrenched him bodily from his dreams. Dark dreams, full of foreboding. He was not sorry to put them behind him. He glanced over at Connie. She was still asleep, a faint smile playing upon her lips.

Talbot heard a gentle tap at the door.

"Who is it?" he asked.

"Quiet! You mustn't wake the Baron. It's me, sir, Klove. I've got to speak with you, urgent."

Talbot crossed the room, wrenched the chair from under the handle and opened the door. Klove stood glancing up and down the corridor nervously, wringing his hands. At Talbot's invitation he stepped into the room and closed the door, taking care to make as little noise as possible.

"Good God, man, what's happened to your face? Did the Baron do this to you?"

Klove shrugged dismissively.

"It's of no consequence, young Master," he said, looking at his shoes, "but you must listen to me. You and Miss Constance is in terrible danger, sir," he muttered into the carpet, "the Baron, sir, he... Well, he..."

"Come on - what did you say your name was again, friend?"

"Klove, sir."

"Come on, Klove, out with it - your master may be a scoundrel and a bully, but I won't bite."

"Well, sir, he wants Miss Constance for his own, like," muttered Klove, blushing furiously.

"Oh, he does, does he?" growled Talbot, "I thought he was looking at her strangely - "

" - Who was looking at me, Larry?"

218

Talbot and Klove turned shocked faces towards the bed. Constance was awake. She yawned and stretched decorously.

"Connie!" Talbot rushed to her side and fervently clasped her hand. Constance touched him on the cheek, and they kissed. Klove looked away. After what seemed, in Klove's judgment, an improperly long time, their lips parted. Talbot sat back on the bed and gazed into his fiancé's eyes.

"Connie, do you know where you are?"

Constance looked around the room.

"Is it the castle? Castle Dracula?"

Talbot shook his head.

"I'm sorry, Larry," she continued, "I remember climbing up the hillside with the others, and meeting that nice Mr. Renwick outside the castle. But everything after that is a blank. How did I get here? Where is Ajax?"

Talbot lowered his eyes. Constance gripped his arm.

"What has happened to my brother? Where are Victoria and Ferdinand? Tell me!"

Talbot looked back up at her, his eyes welling with tears.

"Dead, Connie, they're all dead," he said at last. Constance let out a muted cry and clapped her hand to her mouth.

"No!" she cried, "They can't be! You're wrong...I-I was with them!" Talbot put his hands on Constance' shoulders. She struggled against him for a moment, as if by freeing herself from his grasp she might free herself from the meaning of his words. Then the tears came, and she collapsed back into his arms.

After a decent pause, Klove coughed.

"I knows as you're dreadful upset and all, Miss, but - "

" - Of course, Klove," said Talbot, "you are right."

"Connie, you must listen to me. We are in the castle of Baron Frankenstein. As Ferdinand had feared, Frankenstein will not help me: indeed, according to his manservant here, he intends to do us great harm. We must make our escape now, while he sleeps.

"Klove, will you show us the way out?"

"Better'n that, sir; I'll come with you. I've got no place here any more. If I was to stay on after you'd gone, the Master would hold me responsible for letting you escape. He'd kill me, for sure."

Talbot slapped the young manservant on the shoulder.

"Good man. We'll throw in our lot together. Connie, are you strong enough to stand?"

Constance wiped away her tears on the back of her hand, and sniffed.

"Of course," she replied, forcing a smile, "and to walk as fast and as far as either of you. But you must give me a minute..."

She nodded delicately in the direction of the dressing table upon which her clothes were laid out.

Once again Klove flushed with embarrassment.

"I-I've got to put a bundle together," he stammered, "and I'll get some stuff from the kitchen - we've a stiff climb ahead of us. I'll be back presently."

* * *

By the time Klove returned to the bedchamber Miss Quigley was up and dressed. The pallor of her complexion contrasted shockingly against the bitter chocolate of her cape. Nevertheless, she wore a brave face and was in the middle of scolding Talbot for fussing over her when the young manservant walked in.

220

He carried two bundles; the first, tied to his staff, contained his few meagre belongings: a shirt, some hose, a pair of old boots and a battered bible his mother had given him. To these he had added the Baron's telescope and syringe set, and a small bottle of morphine. Might as well be hung for a sheep as a lamb, he had reasoned, though he had no intention of being hung for either.

The second bundle held bread, a piece of sausage and a bottle of wine, all wrapped in a white tablecloth. Klove handed it to Talbot.

"Are you ready, Miss?"

Constance nodded bravely.

"Right then; we'd better be off."

They crept out into the corridor, and headed for the stairs.

As they passed through the lofty Baronial hall, Talbot glanced warily at the deerhounds stretched out on the hearth.

"No need to worry about them, Master," muttered Klove.

Talbot looked again. One lay in a pool of dark blood. The hilt of a dagger stuck out of the other's throat. Constance put her hand to her mouth to suppress a cry.

"Damned fool!" hissed Talbot, "why didn't you cover them up?"

Klove shrugged.

"Sorry, Master, Miss; I s'pose I've seen so many horrors in this place that I'm just used to 'em."

At the far end of the hall Klove grasped the iron rings of the doors with both hands and twisted. With a louder clangour than any of them would have wished the latch lifted and the doors swung open.

They blinked in the unaccustomed daylight. A stiff breeze blew into the hall, making Constance shiver.

With calculated deliberation the courtyard had been left to become overgrown and desolate. Rubble from the crumbling walls lay where it had fallen; nor had Frankenstein made any attempt to restore those wings of the castle which had been destroyed by fire. From any distance, the whole structure seemed unoccupied and abandoned, as had been the Baron's intention.

From the ivy-grown stable block came the whinny of a horse anticipating breakfast. Klove chuckled. It struck him how satisfying it would be to make their escape on Frankenstein's own prized pair of black Arab mares. Coincidentally, it would lend them speed and hamper the Baron in his pursuit, a thought that pleased him even more.

"Wait here," he hissed, and made his way across the courtyard. Talbot and Constance watched him disappear into the stables.

"Come on, Come on," muttered Talbot through clenched teeth. Constance squeezed his hand, silently imploring him to patience.

A shot rang out from the building behind them. Chippings flew off the wall a few feet to their right and a bullet ricocheted across the courtyard. Talbot looked up and saw Frankenstein, purple with rage, leaning out of his bedroom window. His revolver was levelled at them.

"Move and I'll blast your damned heads off!" the Baron roared down at them.

No matter how good a marksman Frankenstein might claim to be, Talbot knew that over this distance only the luckiest pistol shot would find its mark.

"Over there! Run!" he urged, pointing towards a breach in the outer wall. Without a moment's hesitation, Constance set off.

The Baron fired again. Talbot ducked, then dashed for the wall, following in Constance's footsteps.

Klove, who had just emerged from the stables leading the horses, saw them disappearing through the gap in the wall. Another gunshot rang out and a puff of dust rose from the ground beside his feet.

Panicked by the gunfire, the horses reared. Klove struggled to keep a hold on their reins, but finally could only watch helplessly as they broke free and galloped out through the main gate.

With gunshots and the frenzied oaths of his former employer echoing around the walls, Klove bolted across the courtyard towards the gap.

Chapter 25

Pretorius stood in the graveyard in the dark, stamping the cold from his feet and feeling foolish. He lifted up his lantern and took another look at the mummified remains on the tombstone nearby, surrounded now by the ritual objects that Dominique had laid out for the ritual.

In the face of Dominique's earnest persuasion, Pretorius' initial scepticism had given way to a faint, desperate hope that there might just be something in what she claimed to be able to do. He was a firm adherent to the belief that in magic and witchcraft there was often a kernel of hermetic truth.

But faced with the crumbling bones on the slab before him, he could not bring himself to believe that any power on earth could return the faintest spark to them.

Joachim trudged across the unkempt grass, wheeling another barrowload of faggots before him. Stopping beside the impressive heap of wood he had already made, he upended the barrow, adding his load to the pyre. Nodding glumly at Pretorius, he headed back towards the house. Pretorius wished that the manservant would hurry up and light it. He blew on his hands.

The doctor knew that there was no way that he could abandon the cold night for the warmth of the library without grievously offending Dominique. And whilst he was not known for allowing other people's feelings to stand in the way of his own freedom of thought and action, this was a different matter. Dominique was not people.

In fact, Pretorius had come to regard her and Joachim as something close to family. Any hope that Dominique had kindled within him that he might soon be in a position to win his wager had been tempered by an anxiety that he would also be saying farewell to his best friends. Given the state of the thing Joachim had dug up, there seemed to be little risk of that. And if friendship demanded that he must stand in a graveyard on a chilly night waiting for a miracle he knew could not happen, then so be it.

Joachim reappeared out of the dark, holding aloft a flaming brand, looking like some giant from the pages of a story. He thrust the torch into the middle of the pile of wood and stood back.

The two watched as flames burst through the faggots and licked up the sides of the bonfire. Pretorius rubbed his hands together.

"That's better, eh?" he said to Joachim.

The manservant, whose mood had not improved, grunted begrudging assent.

"Good. Now we can begin."

The two men turned to see Dominique standing behind them. Pretorius drew a sharp breath.

She wore a flowing robe of a diaphanous white material. From the thrust of her nipples through the fabric, Pretorius realised that she was wearing nothing beneath it.

She carried a snow-white cockerel. It hung upside down, unmoving but for an occasional dejected flap of its outspread wings.

"You understand, Doctor, that you may not divulge anything of what you are about to witness to anybody?"

Pretorius nodded dumbly, trying hard not to look at her breasts.

"Already, by your presence alone, I offend against taboo. To do more would bring unimaginable evil upon our heads."

226

Pretorius inclined his head again. Given the patent impossibility of the task Dominique had set herself, the doctor thought it petty to point out that this promise seemed to rule out any chance of winning his bet.

"You will not need words to convince the Baron. The zombi spell will last long enough for him to witness it for himself."

Pretorius' jaw sagged. Dominique had read his thoughts as clearly as if he had spoken them out loud. This was not the time, however, to be investigating her other mysterious talents.

"You really think that there is some chance of success, then? Even with this?" Pretorius gestured at the pathetic remains on the slab.

Dominique reached out and touched Pretorius on the cheek. The gesture shocked him. When she took her fingers away he continued to feel the impression of her fingers upon his skin as a warm tingle which gradually spread down through his body.

"You will see for yourself, doctor; within the hour."

She held out the cockerel to Joachim, who took it reluctantly, holding it at arm's length, as if it might bear infection. Dominique grasped the hem of her robe and in one swift movement pulled it up and over her head. Her skin glistened in the firelight. Pretorius looked away.

Dominique draped the robe casually over a gravestone.

"You must watch carefully," she said to Pretorius, "everything I do from now on is part of the ritual."

Reluctantly, Pretorius raised his eyes.

Dominique leant over the tombstone, dipped her fingers into a pot containing a greasy red substance, and began to inscribe enigmatic marks and symbols upon her face and torso.

When she was done, she turned to Pretorius and, before he could protest, swiftly daubed his cheeks and forehead. She did the same to Joachim, then turned back to the tombstone and busied herself arranging the containers and utensils she was going to use.

After a while Pretorius realised that she had started to chant: a soft, low, rhythmic sound, coming from deep in her throat, interspersed with yodelling cries and glottal stops. She sang in no language the doctor had ever heard, not even the guttural tongue she used when she spoke to Joachim

She slipped her hand under the skull of the corpse and raised it off the slab a few inches, picked up a ewer and brought the spout to the rags of skin which were all that were left of its lips. Looking for all the world like a nurse ministering to a feeble patient, she tilted the vessel and allowed a little of the contents to trickle into its mouth. Thick green fluid ran over the dry bones and her fingers, and gathered on the slab.

Dipping a small switch into the pool, she flicked droplets of the fluid over the rest of the skeleton. Suddenly, as if in response to some unseen signal, she dug into a bowl, rushed over to the bonfire and threw a handful of herbs into the flames. With a roar the flames belched skyward and changed colour to a livid vermilion, colouring the graves, the grass and the shocked faces of the two men blood-red.

Dominique swayed to the rhythm of her own song. As she whirled past Joachim, she reached out and snatched the cockerel from his hands. Her chanting became more urgent. Sweat glistened on her skin. The bird, stained scarlet in the firelight, flapped its wings wildly.

Then Dominique was spinning across the grass and came to a halt before the tombstone again. Holding the cockerel down on the slab she snatched up a

228

kitchen cleaver and brought it down with shattering force upon the frantic creature's neck. The blade ground sparks from the ancient stone, and the cockerel's head spun across the slab.

Dominique held the thrashing body of the bird over the corpse, letting the blood spurt over the skull and into its mouth and nose. When the flow had ebbed to a trickle, and the cockerel's spasms died away to an occasional twitch, Dominique cast it aside. Her whole body slumped and she leant upon the slab for support. Pretorius could hear her breath coming in exhausted, panting sobs.

She made as if to turn towards the two men, stumbled, and collapsed lifeless to the ground.

* * *

Joachim was on the grass in an instant, cradling Dominique in his arms, and looking beseechingly at Pretorius for reassurance. The doctor squat beside him and took Dominique's pulse.

"It's all right. She's just fainted. Exhaustion, I think. She will recover soon enough. Let's cover her up and get her back to the house."

He stood up to unbutton his overcoat, then stopped, mid-button. Joachim glanced up to see him standing stock-still, staring wide-eyed at the slab. The servant's eyes followed his gaze.

Painfully slowly, the thing on the slab turned its head and stared back. Its jaw worked feebly as if it was trying to speak. Momentarily forgetting Dominique, Joachim leapt to his feet and backed away. Pretorius laid a hand on his shoulder.

"It's all right, Joachim. I don't think it's any danger to us."

Then he scoffed nervously.

"Listen to me! Actually, I haven't got a clue whether it's dangerous or not. But look at it - my God, look at it, Joachim!"

But Joachim was not listening to Pretorius. With tortoise-like deliberation the zombie was struggling to sit upright. Dominique groaned, and stirred. With a wary eye on the zombie, Joachim grasped her by the arms and dragged her clear.

Pretorius finished undoing his buttons and took off his overcoat. He knelt down beside Dominique and laid it over her.

"Dominique! Are you all right? Can you hear me?"

Dominique nodded feebly.

"Dominique it - it's worked!"

Dominique nodded again. The corners of her mouth twitched.

"Now... you... believe me," she murmured, "where is... Joachim?"

Joachim grunted. Dominique turned and looked at him. Her smile broadened. She reached up and touched his cheek.

"We had better get back... to the house. We must... start packing."

"Not tonight, my dear," said Pretorius gently, "you have tomorrow, the next day, and every day of the rest of your lives. But tonight you must rest."

He rose, creaking, to his feet and gazed in silent awe at the creature. Its fingers had discovered the edge of the tombstone, and it was straining to drag itself off the slab.

He was only dimly aware of Joachim's urgent grunting until the manservant grabbed a handful of his shirt sleeve. He stretched out an arm and pointed. Pretorius reluctantly tore his attention from the zombie and turned it in the direction of Joachim's trembling finger.

230

Something had emerged from the woods and was lumbering towards them. It was human in size and shape, but wrapped from head to foot in mouldering cloth. Between the layers of bandage, red eyes gleamed with dull malevolence.

Pretorius raised his arms to protect himself and cried out; but the sound was cut short as the mummy wrapped its hands around his throat and crushed his windpipe. Stars burst before the doctor's eyes. His feet left the ground, leaving him kicking uselessly in mid-air.

Joachim leapt to his master's defence, tearing frantically at the creature's wrists, gouging through cloth and dry skin to no effect. Holding the limp figure of Pretorius aloft in one hand, the mummy drew back its other arm and delivered Joachim a sickening blow that sent him reeling across the grass and into the fringes of the bonfire. Embers scattered across the nearby graves and a cloud of sparks rose up like a firework.

Joachim shook the effects of the blow from his head, pulled a flaming brand from the fire, and plunged it into the mummy's back.

Bey had done all too good a job of drying Kharis out. The fire spread greedily across the tinder-dry bandages and within seconds the monster's body was engulfed in flames. Letting Pretorius limp body fall to the ground, it beat ineffectually at its face and shoulders, succeeding only in transferring the fire to the wrappings on its hands and arms. Joachim stepped back, turning his face from the searing heat. The blazing mummy dropped to its knees, clutching its face in silent agony and fell forward to the grass.

Dominique struggled to her feet and staggered over to where Pretorius' body lay, twisted and unmoving. She bent over him, then turned to Joachim, tears glistening on her cheeks.

"He's dead, Joachim. The Doctor's dead."

Joachim's eyes filled with horror and disbelief. He stretched a beseeching hand towards Dominique, then with silent and awesome majesty collapsed headlong to the ground, the jewel encrusted hilt of a dagger jutting out between his shoulder-blades.

"Thus die the enemies of Isis and Osiris!" hissed Turhan Bey; then turned and vanished into the night.

* * *

Dominique staggered over to Joachim and tried to roll him over; but she was still too weak from her exertions. With a howl of despair she threw herself upon his broad shoulders and sobbed out her grief.

"No! No! No!"

Over and over again she moaned the word into his ear, as if by repeating it she might deny his death and waken him: but she knew better than that. No amount of entreating would restore that which had fled from him.

For one brief moment she was tempted to perform the zombi ritual on him. But in her heart she knew that, while the Ju-ju magic might restore movement to her loved one's limbs, he would be no more truly alive than was the hideous thing on the tombstone.

She looked across at the zombie to witness it drag itself painfully off the edge of the tombstone, only to topple straight into the heart of the dying embers that were all that remained of the mummy. The fire hungrily turned its attentions to the dry, twitching limbs of this new human fuel.

Joachim was dead. The only man she had ever loved had been snatched from her, at the very dawn of a new life together as free man and woman. Gone, too, was the only white man who had ever treated her with decency and respect.

232

They had left her alone in an alien and hostile world; a world of hypocrites and murderers, monsters and worthless, maggot-skinned peasants.

Rage rose within her, until its red mist blinded her and its roaring drowned out all sound. This vile world had destroyed everything that made her life worth living. No vengeance would satisfy her now but to destroy the world in her turn.

She kissed Joachim's hair, once, then clasped the handle of the dagger and wrest it from his back. Blood welled sluggishly from the wound. Dominique dipped a fingertip in the blood, and tasted it.

A dreamy smile played on her face as she strolled out of the light of the fire and stopped in a small clearing. She looked at the ancient graves around her. This would be a fine place.

She began to chant again; a variation on the song she had sung before. As she chanted, she began to turn on her heel; at first slowly, but gaining speed, spinning faster and faster as the tempo of her song increased, until the world became an irrelevance, an abstraction, a dark blur whirling around her.

As the chant built to a crescendo she brought the knife up to her neck. There was no cold shock as she touched the blade against her skin. Joachim had already warmed it for her. He had always been thoughtful like that. Dominique pressed down hard on the blade and drew it across her throat.

Blood sprayed from the gash in a crimson arc, splattering the grass and the gravestones. The knife flew from her hand into the grass. Dominique managed to describe a further three complete revolutions before her consciousness faltered and her body spun out of control. She careered into a headstone, smashing the back of her skull, and slid to the ground, leaving a red trail upon the lichen-encrusted granite.

All was still. The two fires, the fire of dead wood and the pyre of undead flesh, began to die down. The body of Dr. Pretorius lay on its back, staring unblinking into the night sky.

A gentle breeze fanned the flames. A few feathery flakes of ash took to the air and settled on Joachim's broad back.

The corpse of Dominique sat upright, propped against the gravestone. Blood oozed from the wound in her throat and dripped from her nipples onto her legs. All was still.

Then a hand burst out of the ground.

Chapter 26

From his vantage point on the hillside above Karnstein, Michael spotted the bonfire in the graveyard from a couple of miles away. While instinct directed him towards the village and the comforts of the Crow & Gibbet, curiosity turned his feet towards the fire, even though that involved passing through the woods behind the Abbey House.

The moment he plunged into its stygian gloom he regretted his decision. Things hooted and twittered in the dark. Twigs snapped and leaves rustled. Something whooped nearby. Michael puckered his lips and tried to whistle, and failed.

Directly ahead, he heard something large crashing through the undergrowth towards him.

"Oh Gawd!" he whined softly.

He looked around for somewhere to hide. A few yards away was an ancient oak, its thick trunk twisted and ivy-clad with age. He crept over to it and pressed himself into its dark green foliage.

As he emerged from the darkness and passed by, Michael recognised the flower pot head-dress of the man he had seen so fleetingly on Farkle Bridge, the one whom the doctor had called Bey. He was muttering darkly, in foreign, Michael thought. A few yards beyond Michael's hiding place his grumblings gave way to loud oaths, and he flung the flower pot to the ground and kicked it. Then as quickly as he had appeared, the man strode off into the shadows and was gone.

Michael emerged from behind the tree, still fluttery and shaken, but intrigued, nonetheless. Pretorius might be interested to know that the flower pot man had been so near to the Abbey House; if he didn't know already, that is.

As he neared the far side of the wood Michael took comfort in the glow of the fire through the trees. He quickened his pace, emerging finally and with considerable relief into the graveyard. Even then he did not approach the fire openly, but picked his way cautiously from gravestone to gravestone, ducking low and staying hidden until he was near enough to see -

Michael stopped short and rose slowly from his hiding place, gawping slack-jawed at the carnage.

"Christ on a fucking donkey, what's gone off here?" he murmured.

He stepped out from behind the gravestone. His legs seemed to have disappeared from under him, leaving him hovering in mid-air. With no conscious effort he floated into the waning glow of the fires, looking down from his elevation on the corpses of Pretorius and Joachim.

The savage and the doctor, both dead! And another, or was it two? burnt beyond recognition. Michael reached down and touched Joachim's back. The manservant's blood had already started to clot, his flesh to stiffen. Michael rummaged expertly through the doctor's pockets, then looked around for any clues that might throw some light on what had taken place.

Dominique stared out from the shadows, gazing past him towards the Abbey. Michael glided across the grass towards her. He had never seen a savage woman naked before. Come to think of it, he had never seen anyone completely naked, not even himself. Ancient desires whispered to one other in the pit of his stomach; deep in the jungle of his breeches, something stirred.

236

You filthy old twat, he admonished himself, she's bloody dead, she is. Turning away in revulsion, he found himself staring into the empty eye sockets of a mouldering corpse. The undead thing reached out towards him.

Michael turned to flee but found his way blocked by a brace of zombies. They shambled towards him, arms outstretched, mouths working silently. Michael looked over his shoulder. Behind him, hordes of the vile creatures were clambering out of their graves and emerging from the shadows of the gravestones.

Michael felt something grasp his ankle. He looked down. Another zombie was clawing its way out of the earth beneath his legs. Scarcely more than a rotting, muddied skeleton, it clutched his foot with bony fingers and gnawed feebly at his boot.

Michael stumbled backwards, tripped over Dominique's feet and collapsed on top of her. Blood belched from the wound in her throat and spattered the back of his scalp. As he struggled to sit upright her arms came up and closed around his chest.

* * *

It served as a testament to the power of Michael's lungs that Talbot heard his cries from the far side of the wood.

"My God!" he exclaimed, "who's that? Quick, Klove, follow me! Connie, stay here; it may be dangerous."

He set off through the woods at full-tilt, crashing into saplings and stumbling over roots in the dark, unaware that Constance was following close behind him, with Klove reluctantly making up the rear. He burst out of the other side of the woods onto the edge of the graveyard and stood dumbstruck.

Michael had evaded Dominique's clutches and clambered up an ancient and crumbling obelisk. He clung to the top of the grave-marker like a monkey on a stick, bellowing at the top of his voice and looking down fearfully at the throng of undead which milled about below.

Klove finally caught up with the two gentlefolk and came to a halt beside them, gasping for breath. As he took in the scene before them his eyes grew round with astonishment.

"No!" he exclaimed in disbelief, "it can't be!"

Michael looked over his shoulder and recognised the son he had lost so many years ago, unaware that this was the third time in twenty-four hours he had been surprised by the same revelation.

"Klove? Klovey boy is that you?"

Klove nodded his head dumbly.

"But how?" he finally blurted out, "I thought you were - "

It was a miracle. It had to be. In murdering his own father, Klove had committed the most unforgiveable sin of all. But merciful, mysterious God - a God in Whom Klove had ceased to believe a long time ago - had seen fit to resurrect the old bastard. In so doing, had He also absolved Klove of his sin? Was it possible that Klove, too, had been given another crack at redemption? Tears welled in his eyes.

"Praise the Lord!" he exclaimed rapturously, "Glory be! Glory be!"

"Stop blathering, boy, and get these divvils off of me!"

Klove flung his bundle aside and set off across the graveyard with a whoop of righteous indignation. As he passed the site of Joachim's recent excavations, he grabbed the spade and swung it above his head.

The zombie which until a half-hour ago had been Dominique turned at the cry and saw Klove moments before the blade whistled through the air and caught her in the neck, lopping off her head and sending it spinning into the night. Her decapitated body stood for a moment as if awaiting further instructions, then crumpled to the ground, dead for the second and final time.

The other zombies shuffled around to face Klove.

"Who's next, then?" he muttered through gritted teeth.

Oblivious to Klove's challenge, the zombies lurched towards him. Klove swung the spade into the midst of them, slicing the top off one creature's head and catching another in the shoulder.

Before he could strike another blow, a particularly ragged specimen reached out and grasped the spade. Klove twisted and tugged the handle in a macabre tug-of-war, finally recovering the spade with a yank that tore the creature's hand from its wrist and left it still clinging on to the handle. But by then the creatures had him surrounded. Ragged hands pinned his arms to his sides. Hungry mouths yawned before him, revealing rotten teeth.

A moment later Talbot was by his side, tearing the zombies from him and bludgeoning them with a thick branch. Almost as fast as he knocked them to the ground, they clambered ungainly to their feet and attacked again.

"Brain 'em!" instructed Klove.

Talbot directed the full force of his next blow at his assailant's head, caving its skull in and blowing what was left of its eyeballs out of their sockets like corks from a popgun.

Encouraged by his success, Talbot was taking aim at the next available cranium when a steel grip closed around his throat. It was the animate corpse of Joachim, staring blankly ahead through eyes now obscured with a milky-white film. Talbot tried to shout for help, but Joachim's fingers squeezed all sound and all breath from him. The branch fell from his numb fingers. Joachim's face swam before him. Through his ebbing consciousness a loud report rang out.

The side of Joachim's head erupted, spraying a geyser of blood and brains into the air. The undead manservant's grip on Talbot's neck relaxed, and the young American tore himself free. Drawn by the reek of Joachim's blood, the zombies fell upon his fallen body. Within seconds they had ripped open its stomach with their bare hands and were gorging themselves on his intestines.

"Quick! Climb aboard!"

The embattled party looked round. A coach and pair had pulled up on the road outside the graveyard. Two panting bays skittered nervously in the traces, their breath steaming in the light of the coach lamps. Standing atop stood Father Shandor, looking down the sights of a hunting rifle.

"In God's name, move!"

Constance needed no further bidding. She sprinted across the grass, vaulted the wall with impressive ease and clambered into the coach. While most of the zombies were gorging themselves on the remains of Joachim, one or two still stumbled around the base of the obelisk, waiting for Michael's grip to fail. Klove dead-headed them with cold efficiency and tried to attract his father's attention.

"Father!" he shouted, "Get down! We have to get away!"

But by now Michael had worked himself up into such a lather that Klove's words failed to register at all. Klove reached up and grasped his father's ankle. Thinking that he had fallen into the clutches of the undead, Michael redoubled his uproar and tried desperately to shake off his son's grip.

240

Little remained of Joachim to hold the zombies' attention, and those on the fringe of the feeding frenzy began to look around for other sources of meat. Klove realised that filial piety would have to take a back seat if either of them were going to get out of this with their skins on their backs.

"Get down, you daft old pillock!" He roared, and with a mighty heave broke his father's grip on the obelisk. Michael slid down the column and collapsed on top of his son, screaming blue murder and lashing out in all directions. Talbot picked the old man up by the collar and shook him until he quietened down. Klove clambered to his feet, nursing the onset of a second black eye.

The living dead shuffled, staggered and crawled towards them bloody-mouthed and with a hungry glint in their eyes.

Propelling him ahead of them with a succession of encouraging kicks and blows, Klove and Talbot herded Michael across the graveyard towards the waiting coach.

Chapter 27

Like the mycelium of a monstrous fungus, Dominique's final, terrible spell surged through the barren soil of the Vale of Walach. Within minutes it had reached the village and was probing the churchyard, seeking dead flesh upon which to work its dark magic.

* * *

In the Presbytery, Widow Mordant hummed the tune of a favourite hymn as she cleared up after tea. The Father had hardly touched his plate, even though she had cooked his favourite dish. Then, while she was still in the kitchen, he had gone out without as much as a word. It was really quite unlike him; but then, so was much of his behaviour at present.

She picked up the waste paper basket, and heard a telltale clink. Digging a hand into the rubbish she pulled out a brace of empty brandy bottles. She stopped humming, and pursed her lips. This had gone far enough, she thought. She had been making allowances for the Father this last few days, for she appreciated his fears and the extent of his frustration with the Burgomeister. But when he started to hide the evidence of his drinking...

Her unhappy thoughts were interrupted by a hammering at the door.

"All right, all right, I can hear you. Do you want to wake the dead?" she grumbled, as she stumped up the hall.

"Well, what is it?" she asked, flinging open the door.

"Is the Father in?"

It was Old Tom, red-faced and panting, followed close behind by an angry looking stranger in a threadbare crimson uniform, carrying a horn.

"No he's not. What's your business with him, anyway?"

Tom frowned.

"This is the driver of the Prague mail coach. Just now, as he was stepping out of the Crow, someone drove off in his coach. He got a look at who it was: he says it was a priest."

"Big, fierce-looking bugger with a bushy beard," interjected the driver. "Priest or no bloody priest I'd have had a pop at him, only he was waving a rifle about -
"

" - I'll thank you not you use language of that sort," interrupted Widow Mordant, drawing herself up to her full impressive height. "Father Shandor is not in the habit of stealing stagecoaches. If, however, you regularly partake of strong liquor whilst engaged upon your official duties, I am not at all surprised to hear that you have lost the vehicle in your charge. I can only hope that you were carrying no passengers. Good evening."

The Widow managed to keep up her expression of icy dignity until she had slammed the door in the men's faces. Then she leant back against it for support.

A check of the study confirmed her worst fears. The door of the gun cupboard was wide open and the hunting rifle was missing from its place. The room swam around her. She clutched her rosary.

The hammering on the front door started up again.

"For Goodness sake!" she exploded. What did Tom think he was playing at? This time she would really give him a piece of her mind. The Widow strode up to the door and flung it open.

Three pasty-faced corpses in varying stages of decomposition leered at her from the doorstep. On the path behind them several others looked up from the bloody corpses of Tom and the coach driver.

244

For once the Widow Mordant was lost for words.

* * *

Not so very far away, Burgomeister von Trapp was rapping out his secret code on the side door of the Lair again. The side door was the preferred exit of many of the house's clients, particularly those who did not care to acknowledge to others still waiting in the parlour the brevity of their visit upstairs. Only Von Trapp was permitted to use it as an entrance, in exchange for his toleration of the business of the house.

He cursed. What the hell was Nellie up to? It would not do for his weekly visit to the brothel to become public knowledge. He had his position to consider, after all. When, after another long wait, Nellie had still not appeared, he tried the door.

It opened into a short hallway. To one side was the door into the parlour, a door which Nellie left open every Friday night in anticipation of his arrival. Tonight, however, it was shut and locked.

Ahead, a narrow flight of stairs led up to the girls' rooms. Rather than risk drawing attention to himself by knocking at the parlour door, the Burgomeister headed straight up to Elsbieta's room. The stairs were dimly lit and uneven, but he was familiar with the eccentricities of each tread.

A door at the top of the stairs opened onto the landing. Von Trapp pressed an ear to Elsbieta's door and listened for any one of the range of noises which might indicate that she was engaged with a client. He could hear nothing - nothing at all. The landing was eerily silent.

He knocked lightly on the door and slipped through without waiting for a reply. The room was simply furnished, with a rattan chair, a plain washstand and wardrobe, and Elsbieta's old bed, the brass rails of which were polished bright by the countless sweaty hands which had clung on to them over the years. She had decorated the walls with pictures torn from magazines; pictures of elegant society ladies and pretty pastoral scenes.

A screen across one corner of the room afforded a little privacy, though von Trapp could not imagine for a moment what a whore might have left to do in private that she had not done a thousand times under the gaze of others. A single lamp burnt upon the washstand, casting a soft, warm glow over the room.

"Elsbieta?" the Burgomeister hissed. There was no reply.

"Elsbieta?"

Von Trapp heard a grunt from the corner. A sheer black stocking appeared provocatively over the top of the screen.

The Burgomeister relaxed and sat down on the edge of the bed. The springs complained under his weight.

"Saucy mare!" he growled in approval, taking his boots off. "Nellie forgot to leave the connecting door open tonight, stupid cow. You must have a word with her, my dear: I can't be kept waiting in the street."

The Burgomeister continued his one-sided conversation with the unseen Elsbieta as he undressed and lay back naked on the bed. Hidden from his view by the hairy hemisphere of his stomach, the sceptre of his passion drummed impatiently against his belly button.

Von Trapp heard movement behind the screen, and Elsbieta's last item of underclothing was flung over the top. He closed his eyes in anticipation.

"It's been the very devil of a week. I'm tense in every sinew; I need to relax."

He heard Elsbieta emerge from behind the screen and slowly cross the room. He wiggled his toes with delight.

246

"So I fancy something a bit special tonight. Nibble me, Elsbieta."

Von Trapp felt her weight on the edge of the bed. Fingers closed around his winkle.

"Bloody hell, woman! Your hands are freezing!"

The Burgomeister opened his eyes. He just caught a glimpse of Elsbieta's blank expression and the clouded eyes of the newly undead, before her face disappeared like the setting sun behind the rolling mound of his stomach.

His screams rang through the brothel like a dinner gong, summoning the zombies from every room.

* * *

"For Christ's sake, hurry!" roared John the Smith, throwing every ounce of his weight against the door of the Crow and Gibbet. Yeoman Muller swept a cascade of steins and glasses off the nearest trestle, dragged it across the room and wedged it under the door handle.

"That won't keep them out," whined Bumblewicz from the corner of the room. Tears matted his eyelashes, and his nose was running. He counted the beads of his wife's rosary with trembling fingers.

"Nothing can keep them out. We're all going to die!"

As if to illustrate his point, a pair of skeletal arms burst through one of the windows and made a grab for Granny Blepp.

Yeoman Woblinz dragged the old woman out of harm's way and brought his dagger down on the nearest of the clawing hands, pinning it to the windowsill. The zombie's head appeared through the window, looked down vexedly at its impaled hand, and then directed a baleful stare at Woblinz. In the absence of any other weapon, Woblinz drove his fist into its face. The front of its skull caved in, and Woblinz' fist plunged into the foul matter within.

247

Its central nervous system destroyed, the zombie collapsed over the windowsill like a puppet with its strings cut. Woblinz struggled to extract his fist from the ruins of the creature's head, gouging several deep cuts in his hand on the jagged edges of its shattered skull.

Smith and Muller dragged another trestle across the room.

"Are you all right, Bert?" asked Muller, as they up-ended it over the window.

"Just a scratch," dismissed Woblinz, wiping blood and slime onto his breeches.

"Look!" shouted Gimmer Schwab from behind the bar. He held up a hammer. "There's nails, too, and wood; lots of it."

Muller helped Schwab carry a load of timber over to the window. Woblinz and the Smith started nailing battens across the trestle.

"Nails and wood won't stop 'em," blubbed Bumblewicz, "sooner or later they'll get us all."

"Will someone shut him up!" roared Smith over his shoulder, moving on to the door.

Granny Blepp hobbled towards Bumblewicz.

"Pull yourself together, Bumblewicz! You always were a snivelling little coward. You're meant to be the village carpenter; you - "

A trapdoor in the floor burst open in front of Granny Blepp and a dozen ragged hands reached out for her ankles. Without time even to utter a scream she was dragged into the darkness.

"They've got into the cellar!" shouted Muller, throwing himself upon the trap before any of the horrors could emerge. A hand, caught in the trapdoor, wriggled like an upturned spider an inch from Muller's face. He reared back in horror and the hand was withdrawn. The trapdoor slammed shut beneath him.

Smith hurried over with an armful of wood.

"What about Blepp?" asked Muller.

Something beat on the trapdoor with awesome strength, lifting him several inches off the floor.

"It's too late to save her," shouted Smith, adding his weight to Muller's. "Hurry up, Woblinz! We can't hold the trap down much longer!"

Woblinz staggered across to the two men and looked at them, bleary-eyed.

"You'd better do it," he mumbled, dropping the hammer and nails beside the trapdoor, "I don't feel too good."

He crumpled to the ground and lay still.

"Christ! That's all we need!" muttered Muller, laying a batten across the bucking trapdoor. Smith picked up the hammer and started pounding nails into the wood.

It took a dozen pieces of timber and a hundred nails before Muller and Smith were satisfied that the trapdoor was secure. Smith rolled onto his back and wiped the sweat from his brow. Muller leant over Woblinz' body and searched for a pulse.

"I can't feel anything," he said, looking under Woblinz' eyelid for any sign of life. "I think he's dead."

Smith's reply was cut short by the crash of shattering glass and splintering wood as a zombie burst through the far window. Before he could get out of its way, it had wrapped its arms around Gimmer Schwab and sunk its yellow teeth into his face. Blood spurted onto the walls.

Smith and Muller leapt to their feet and rushed to Schwab's aid. Smith tore the creature off the old man and hurled it to the ground, leaving Muller to beat out its brains with a length of timber.

Schwab remained upright, swaying like a sapling in the wind. His upper jaw was visible through a gaping hole in his cheek: blood soaked his shirtfront, transforming it from coarse linen to lustrous scarlet satin. His breath came in hoarse, irregular gasps. Smith laid the old man down on the floor.

"This'll make a good tale," whispered Schwab, and died in Smith's arms.

Meanwhile, Bumblewicz was staring wide-eyed in horror from his corner at the body of Woblinz. With the slow deliberation of an awakening reptile it raised its head and seemed to wink one milky eye at the joiner. It rose to its feet, grasped the iron ring of the trapdoor, and without any perceptible effort ripped it off its hinges.

Smith looked up from the body of the old man to see foul hordes of the living dead surging up through the trapdoor into the room. Then Schwab's hand closed around his throat, cheating him of his final oath.

Chapter 28

Standing on the footplate, Father Shandor cracked his whip over the horses' flanks, urging them on to greater speed. Beside him, Talbot clung on to the handrail for grim life. The post coach hurtled through the village, crushing beneath its wheels any zombie too slow to get out of its way.

As they passed the Crow and Gibbet, Talbot caught a glimpse of Muller through the window, laying about himself with a wooden spar. Talbot tugged on Shandor's sleeve.

"Shouldn't we stop and try to help, Father?" he shouted above the clatter of the horses' hooves.

"Too many of them!" returned Shandor. Even through the rushing wind, Talbot could smell the brandy on the priest's breath.

"The only way to stop the evil is to seek out and destroy the root of it all."

"And where is that?" asked Talbot.

"Up there!" Shandor pointed with the whip, up the mountainside to where Talbot could see the black bulk of Castle Dracula silhouetted against the night. A shiver ran down his spine.

In the passenger seats, Constance, Klove and Michael bounced around like peas in a drum.

"W-where are we h-heading?" Constance managed to stammer. Klove shrugged.

"S-search me. Away from those e-evil b-bastards, anyway, b-begging your pardon Ma'am."

At that moment the back wheel struck a pot-hole and threw Michael head first into Miss Quigley's lap. He emerged from her skirts eventually with all due expressions of regret, but unable to contain a lascivious grin. Klove nudged his father angrily. Constance shrank back in her seat and stared out of the window.

Glass exploded into the carriage as a pair of long-dead arms burst through the window and lunged at Constance. Clawed fingers entwined themselves in her hair and dragged her towards the open window.

Klove leapt to her aid, gouging strips of dead skin from the zombie's wrists as he struggled to break its grip, but to no avail. The creature thrust its head through the broken window and snapped at Klove's ear. Klove fell back into the well between the seats.

Constance was so close to the creature's gaping maw that she could see the worms burrowing under its tongue. Then a metal barrel appeared outside the window and tapped the zombie on the shoulder. It looked up.

Talbot squeezed the trigger of the Father's rifle. The blast blew the zombie's head off its shoulders. It flew though the air, hit the road and bounced after the coach for several yards, as if even decapitation was not going to deter it from its meal. Its hands relaxed their hold on Constance's, and the body fell off the side of the coach and was swallowed up by the night.

Constance collapsed back onto her seat with powder burns on her cheek and the shot still ringing in her ears. Klove clambered up off the floor.

Michael fished about in his pocket and produced Pretorius' hip flask.

"Bugger almost had you there," he said, taking a nip and then offering the flask to Constance.

"And why the hell didn't you try to help?"

Michael shrugged non-committally. Constance snatched the flask from him, drained it in one, and threw it out of the window.

* * *

In no time the coach had left the village far behind and the track deteriorated still further. All attempts at conversation were abandoned as everybody concentrated on staying on board.

At last the grim crenellations of Castle Dracula appeared before them. The drawbridge had not been raised nor the portcullis lowered since Talbot's hasty departure. Without letting up speed, Shandor directed the horses between the gateposts.

"For Christ's sake, Shandor, it won't take our weight!" shouted Talbot, ducking low in his seat.

The horses' hooves thundered over the rotten planks and the wheels of the coach clattered behind. For a moment Talbot thought that they were going to make it after all. Then a plank collapsed beneath them and the back axle shattered, leaving one of the back wheels wedged between the ancient boards. Their momentum and the exertions of the horses was enough to see them through the portcullis and into the courtyard, trailing splinters and sparks. The coach jack-knifed, threatening to collide with the horses, and ground to a halt in a cloud of dust. Shandor leapt down to the ground.

Talbot and Constance dismounted from the coach and stood beside the Father. The courtyard was quiet and still. Only the snorting of the horses disturbed the silence. The dust settled slowly around them.

"Well, what now?" asked Constance.

"Now you come with me, my dear," came a silky voice from behind them.

They spun around. Baron Frankenstein stepped out of the shadow of the gatehouse. He held his revolver at waist height, aimed at Shandor.

"Put the gun down, please, Father. I knew that you would turn up here eventually if I waited long enough. He really is extremely clever at getting what he wants."

"Who is clever at getting what?" asked Shandor, throwing his rifle aside.

"Count Dracula, you fat old fool! Did you think you had come here of your own free will? You have been a puppet in his hands. He has just been manipulating you to get his hands on the girl."

Michael and Klove had dismounted from the far side of the coach, and had remained there, out of sight, when the Baron had announced his presence. Now, Michael tapped Klove on the shoulder.

"C'mon Klovey boy; there's a door open over there," he whispered, pointing to a black void in the castle wall. "We can make it without him spotting us if we keeps our heads down."

"No, father," replied Klove, "we can't leave Miss Constance and the others."

"Ballocks we can't!" hissed Michael. "This is no quarrel of our'n, son. I'm going anyway, with you or without; so what's it going to be?"

But the sibilant hiss of the pair's quarrel had attracted Frankenstein's attention. He pointed the pistol into the shadow of the coach.

"Who's there? Come on, show yourself"

"Go on then, dad, get away while you can." Klove muttered to his father, and stepped out into the moonlight with his hands raised.

"Why, Klove, what an unexpected surprise. So good of you to join us. Now get over there with the others.

"Where was I? Ah, yes, Dracula. You see, our friend the Count has a particular affection for Miss Quigley, and would take her for his bride - one of them, anyway.

254

But he reckoned without me, I'm afraid. So, before you all wake him up with your antics I'll just take the girl and be on my way."

Talbot placed himself between Frankenstein and Constance.

"Over my dead body," he said.

"Yes, I'm glad you brought that up" replied Frankenstein, and fired.

Talbot cried out and clutched his arm. Blood trickled between his fingers.

"Since you described the nature of your malady to me I have done a little background reading on lycanthropy. It has really quite intrigued me, and I am delighted to be able to take this opportunity to study the symptoms. I gather that they can be induced through stress."

He fired again. Blood spurted from the back of Talbot's thigh. He collapsed to one knee. Shandor made a move towards his rifle and caught a bullet in the gut. He fell to the ground, clutching his stomach.

"Please don't be tiresome. I can't afford to waste bullets. There are only two left in the chamber before the silver one. A silver bullet would be fatal to your fiancé, would it not, Miss Quigley?

"Or perhaps you would rather I spared him the last bullet? You would? It's perfectly simple: all you have to do is to break off your engagement with him and leave with me. The choice is yours, Miss Quigley - Constance - either break his heart yourself, or trust me to do it for you."

Constance stepped out from behind Talbot. She wrenched the ring from her engagement finger.

"No!" Talbot cried, clutching her skirt.

Constance knelt down beside her fiancé and prised his fingers open, then pressed the ring into his palm.

"You know how much I love you, Larry. Without you, life would have no meaning. This way, at least I will know that you are still alive."

She stood back up.

"Very well, Baron. I will come with you on the condition that you spare the lives of my friends."

"As you wish, my dear. Now we must make haste; our horses await us outside."

Ignoring Talbot's helpless protests, Constance walked slowly over to the Baron and took his proffered hand.

"Stop!" The command rolled around the castle walls like thunder. Even Shandor, in his agony, raised his head and looked.

A majestic figure strode out of the dark, his cloak billowing around him like a scarlet halo. He was tall and stately, and in his angular, handsome features, the Father saw as much dignity as evil, nobility as well as depravity. He struggled against a blasphemous urge to venerate the magnificent creature before him.

Count Dracula raised his arm and levelled a finger at the Baron.

"I told you before, the girl is mine!"

Frankenstein's eyes flashed in rage; but when he spoke, Shandor detected a crack in his voice.

"And I told you she is not! What makes you think that you can just take everything you damn well like, eh? You may scare these superstitious peasants, but you don't scare me!"

In one swift movement the Baron pulled Constance to him, thrust his hand into her cleavage and pulled out her crucifix.

Dracula hissed furiously, averting his eyes from the accursed sight.

256

"And now, if you will excuse me, I'll be on my way. You are welcome to these fellows, old chap, but take care not to break a tooth on the bullets in them. I advise you not to follow after me, however. You will find me more than prepared for you."

Frankenstein patted the satchel that hung by his side.

He started to back away through the gate, holding Constance like a shield in front of him; but as he passed the gatehouse, four of Dracula's harem burst out of the door. Before he could even turn they had overwhelmed him. Serpentlike fangs punctured his throat.

Constance tore herself out of the Baron's arms, leaving her crucifix and broken chain in his grasp. Frankenstein pressed the silver cross into the face of his nearest attacker.

Talbot heard the sizzle of burning flesh. The bride screamed in agony and slapped the cross from the Baron's hand; then tore into his neck with the fury of a virago. Frankenstein sank slowly to the ground. Talbot caught one last sight of him, ashen-faced and silently pleading; then he was gone, buried under the writhing mound of feasting vampires.

"Miss Constance!"

Talbot turned at Klove's cry.

Bereft of the protection of the cross, Constance had fallen prey once more to the full force of Dracula's will. Transfixed by his mesmeric gaze, she was being drawn irresistibly towards him.

Dracula grasped the shoulder of her dress and tore it away. Constance did not flinch.

Talbot tried to stand, but fell back onto his knees, crying out aloud in pain and frustration. He squeezed tears of pain from his eyes.

"No!" he cried out in despair, "not now!"

But no matter how hard he blinked, the familiar red mist was creeping inexorably over his vision.

* * *

Michael leant over the parapet of the watchtower, observing events below with an uneasy combination of guilt and detachment. A spear, selected for its length and ferocity from the display in the Great Hall, leaned against the balustrade beside him.

What concern was it to him if the fools down below chose to throw their lives away? He didn't owe them nothing. True, the young Master had saved his life; and granted, Shandor was never slow with a florin; and Miss Squiggly, or whatever she was called, well, at least she had a fine pair of knockers. But as long as Klove kept his head down, the devil could take the rest of them. And it looked as though he was about to do just that.

As he watched Dracula bend over the bare neck of Constance, however, Michael was horrified to see his son leap to her aid. Thrusting the woman aside, Klove drew a dagger from under his smock and plunged it into the vampire's chest.

Michael cupped his hand to his mouth.

"Run, Klovey boy!" he shouted, waving frantically. "For God's sake get away from him!"

But either Klove could not hear, or chose to disobey him, or was incapable of movement. He remained rooted to the spot as Dracula grasped the dagger and pulled it slowly from his chest. He grasped Klove by the shoulder in a gesture which, from Michael's vantage point, looked almost fraternal, then drove the

258

knife deep into the lad's stomach. He twisted the blade viciously, twice, then released him.

Klove dropped to his knees, clutching his stomach, and fell silently onto his face.

High above, Michael shook his head in hopeless denial.

It couldn't be. Not now, not when he and Klove had just discovered each other again after so many years. There was so much that Michael needed to make up for, so many things the two of them had yet to do together. A tear rolled down his cheek for all the things that now would never be.

He felt anger surge through him in a hot flood not entirely dissimilar to the familiar sensation of wetting himself. He swung the spear against one of the pillars, sending the steel head and the end of the shaft spinning into the night. But the rage kept swelling within him until it had filled him up and there was nowhere left for it to go. Except down. With a cry of anguish and fury, Michael ran towards the parapet and launched himself over the side.

* * *

Shrieking like a valkyrie, Michael plunged out of the sky. Everybody looked up, even Dracula. He caught a momentary glimpse of the splintered end of the spear in Michael's hands and raised an arm to protect himself. The wooden shaft pierced his hand and entered his body through his mouth, passed through every major organ including his heart and burst out of his groin, pinning him upright to the ground like a moth on a cork.

Michael tumbled over Dracula's body and hit the ground, head first. His arm flopped across Klove's shoulders, and remained there.

The Count's free arm flailed wildly. Blood trickled from his mouth, nose and eyes, and ran down the shaft of the spear. His skin began aging visibly, first wrinkling, then turning dry and desiccated and flaking away like ash. He arched his head back and roared defiance at the night sky, a cry that died away to a hoarse croak and gurgle. When he returned his furious gaze to the mortals standing paralysed before him, his eyes were the colour of blood.

Wisps of steam were now curling from beneath his collar and cuffs. He opened his mouth again, but as he did, the flesh shrank from his face, exposing the bone of his jaw and skull. The eyes shrivelled in their sockets and his body half-slumped, half crumbled to the ground.

A minute later, all that remained of the immortal Count was a pile of grey dust.

Seeing the body of their undead lover rotting away before their eyes, the Brides howled in collective lament. They looked round for a scapegoat upon whom to avenge their master's death, and settled upon Constance with eyes full of animal hatred.

Chapter 29

Dawn was breaking over the castle.

Despite the bodies that littered the courtyard, the ravens were not breakfasting at Castle Dracula this morning. They were far below, in the village, where the pickings were richer still.

Constance finished bandaging Father Shandor's stomach and helped him to his feet.

"The shot seems to have gone clean through you without damaging any of the vital organs," she said. "You were lucky, Father."

Father Shandor looked around the courtyard and nodded his head.

"I was," he agreed.

Talbot limped from the stables, carrying a saddle. Constance clicked her tongue in exasperation.

"You shouldn't be lifting anything in your state!" she scolded, taking the saddle from him.

Talbot stood beside Shandor, and both watched Constance saddle the second horse.

"Will you come with us?" asked Talbot.

"Where are you going?" asked Shandor.

Talbot shrugged.

"There must be somebody, somewhere who can cure me," he said.

"Us," corrected Constance over her shoulder.

"What's that?" asked Talbot, turning too sharply for his many wounds. He gave an involuntary grunt of pain. Constance winced in sympathy.

"Someone who can cure us," she repeated, hitching up her sleeve and displaying four parallel scratches on her arm. "You clawed me last night."

Talbot looked so mortified that Constance had to smile.

"Oh, you didn't mean to. I just got in your way while you were tearing up the vampire women in your condition. My whole arm is tingling this morning, and the feeling is spreading. I'm certain that I have caught the infection."

Talbot did not look reassured.

"I don't regret it, Larry, not for a moment," she said, "After all, it means that there is no longer any need for us to travel separately. And no impediment to our marriage."

"I will pray for you," said Shandor. "God knows, you will need it. But I cannot accompany you. I must return to the village. There will be many bodies to bury."

"Aren't you afraid?" asked Constance.

"What is there left to be frightened of? I have seen too much to be afraid any more."

"We will help you bury Klove and Michael before we go," said Talbot "It's the least we can do. After all, the old man saved us all in the end, didn't he? I would like to say my farewell to him - "

"Haven't you noticed?" asked Shandor, pointing over to where Dracula's cape rippled lazily in the breeze, pinned to the ground by the broken spear. "Michael's body has disappeared."

For a moment Talbot wondered how and where, but it was only one more mystery to add to last night's litany of inexplicable horrors. He just hoped that the old reprobate had found some kind of peace.

Chapter 30

Christopher Lee dwarfed Michael Ripper. At six foot four, he stood a full nine inches taller than his companion. The two stood shoulder to elbow on a platform behind one of the fibreglass parapets, watching the cast & crew in the courtyard below record the last few takes of the scene and, indeed, the film.

Ripper looked up at his friend. Although Lee's gaze was still directed towards the stage, he was no longer seeing the hubbub below.

"Penny for your thoughts?" Ripper asked.

Lee glanced at him and smiled.

"Nothing very coherent," he replied apologetically. "I was wondering where we go from here. Not you and I – we'll soldier on, whatever happens – but the movies. It seems to me that fantastic film – I prefer that to 'horror', which seems so limiting and crass – is trapped in a sucking pit of sensationalism."

"I couldn't agree more," replied Ripper. "I was saying something of the kind to Roy just the other day, though not as eloquently. Oliver didn't agree."

"He wouldn't; Mister Reed is a creature of the pop culture and good for him, I suppose. He regards the film industry as a giant party and his greatest challenge is in seeing how many taboos he can break and how many girls he can bed.

"But I am a conservative, Michael, in every sense of the word, and not ashamed of it. It seems to me to be a fundamental principle of civilisation and of culture that we should conserve that which we believe to be right, or which has proven itself through service to be useful. Conserve it, and build upon it: that is how civilisation grows, from generation to generation.

"But there is a revolutionary fervour – and when I say 'revolutionary', frankly I mean socialist and perhaps even anarchistic - to tear down everything that is established, refined and beautiful and to replace it with sensationalism, brutality and ugliness.

"Have you seen The Night of the Living Dead?"

The question caught Ripper by surprise. He shook his head. "Though it's stirred up such a rumpus, I feel I should," he added.

"Don't bother," said Lee, "it's an hour and a half of sadistic nihilism. It scarcely has a story – not in the sense that you or I would understand the word, anyway. There is nothing in it to uplift, or even to entertain, and the ending is a testament to despair. It's an ugly film."

Ripper whistled softly.

"But apart from that, did you like it?" he asked, with a grin.

"And the worst of it is, I believe it's the future," Lee continued. "Sometimes I see all this -" he swept a hand across the set below "– as something of a gothic revival. And if I'm being too generous in that, then at the very least it's been a damned good story factory.

"But have you seen the script for *Taste the Blood*? The breasts are out, in lieu of a story worth a damn. And why? It doesn't take a Freud to recognise that the vampire's bite is symbolic of the sex act. But by making it literal, you diminish it.

"And it's the same with violence: the implicit is so much more effective than the explicit because, as they say, the pictures are better. It doesn't take much to imply an horrific death: the flash of a razor; the look of horror in the prospective victim's eyes; a scream cut short and bingo! More terrifying than any amount of prosthetics and gore.

264

"Perhaps I'm getting old. Of course I'm getting old! We all are. Even Ollie."

They stood in silence for a moment. Then Ripper recalled the story that had evaded him in the café a couple of days ago.

"Chris," he said, "Do you remember once telling me some Chinese legend involving a king and a butterfly?"

Lee smiled. He closed his eyes.

"The Emperor Chong Soo fell asleep," he recited from memory, "and dreamt that he was a butterfly. When he awoke he did not know whether he, Chong Soo, had been dreaming that he was a butterfly, or whether he was a butterfly, dreaming that he was Chong Soo."

"Confucius?" asked Ripper, whose knowledge of Chinese philosophy and literature was limited, effectively, to that one name. Lee shook his head.

"The Book of Chong Soo," he said. "One of the three classic Taoist texts."

"It implies, presumably, that life is an illusion?" asked Ripper. Lee turned his head to his companion and considered him with affection and respect.

"Or perhaps that we are not equipped to tell whether it is illusory or not," he replied. "Why do you ask?"

"No reason," Ripper replied, turning his attention back to the cast and crew far below.

Epilogue

Michael woke up coughing. He sat up in bed and spat on the floor. The roof of his mouth was as dry as dusty death. He reached for the bottle on the floor and swallowed the last dregs of gin.

Thus fortified, he climbed out of bed and stood up. He had neglected to undress before going to sleep and his skirt was crumpled, and twisted round his waist. He dragged the waistband back to vaguely the right position and flattened down the creases.

He lifted the curtain away from the window and peered out through the cracked and grimy panes. It was late and a thin fog had descended, softening the harsh edges of the alleyway.

He scratched his tits, picked up a moth-eaten shawl from the chair and draped it around his shoulders, then opened the door and stepped out into the night.

At the end of the alley he turned on to Artillery Row. It was gone turning-out time, but an optimistic newspaper boy still lingered on the street corner, trying to interest the drunks in his last few copies of the evening rag.

"Read all abaht it!" he bellowed in an unlikely cockney accent. "Second bloody murder in Whitechapel! Police baffled! Read all abaht it!"

But Michael was not interested. Until he found a bit of business he didn't have the price of a paper. And he couldn't read anyway.

In the gloom beyond the next lamp-post he saw a likely prospect. A proper gentleman, in a beaver hat and cape, carrying a cane. His face was hidden under the shadow of his topper, but as far as Michael was concerned he could look like Quasimodo as long as he had money and was willing to be parted from it for a bit of how's-your-father.

He brushed back a wisp of hair, assumed the toothless gawp that he considered his most alluring expression and sauntered casually towards the stranger.

Printed in Great Britain
by Amazon

27183295R00149